"The price of apathy towards public affairs is to be ruled by evil men"

Platon

Andreas Geiger (ed.)
**EU Lobbying Handbook –
A guide to modern
participation in Brussels**

1st edition
© Helios Media GmbH,
Berlin 2006

Helios Media GmbH
Friedrichstraße 209
D – 10969 Berlin
Tel.: + 49 (0) 30 / 84 85 90
Fax: + 49 (0) 30 / 84 85 92 00
www.helios-media.com

Editorial staff: Sandra Amorim,
Horst Jürgen Krämer
Cover: Petra Czechowski
Typeset and Layout:
Franziska Söhner

Printed in Germany by
Print & Media

ISBN: 3–9811316–06

EU Lobbying Handbook

A guide to modern participation in Brussels

Andreas Geiger

Content

The European Union

- Member States of the European Union
- New Member States as of 1 January 2007
- Candidate countries

Preface

There are currently 5,700 regulations and 1,800 directives implemented on EU level. Those numbers, compared with the amount of EU Member States' national laws, are not huge. However, those European legislative acts have a tremendous effect on Member States' national legislative systems. While the regulations can be compared to national laws, the directives have the nature of frame laws which have to be transposed to the Member States' national legislative system. This is the reason why almost half of the national law of each Member State consists of EU law or is at least strongly influenced by it. In the sector of commercial law, this number actually amounts to almost two thirds.

In addition, there are many administrative decisions (mostly from the European Commission) and large amounts of binding and groundbreaking rulings from the European Court of Justice that must be obeyed by the Member States' administrations and courts. The European Court of Justice has further declared that even in those policy areas which are (still) under the sole competence of the Member States, they must take EU law and the legal principles developed by the European Court of Justice into account when using their competencies. Due to this situation, EU lobbyists see themselves confronted with a large playing ground when articulating their interests in the context of EU law and decision making. And they would also be well advised to know the relevant rulings of the European Court of Justice when doing so, in order to acknowledge the limitations of their arguments and forsee their possible success.

However, lobbying generally has a bad reputation in Europe. The layman usually associates it to influential business circles blackmailing decision makers or even to financially powerful albeit sinister organisations bribing legislators. Luckily enough, reality does look different. Without a doubt lobbyists do represent certain interests – and rightfully so. All the better if they are able to do so on only two sheets of paper. But if they do, demanding is not enough. A good lobbyist should be of some help to the decision maker. He should be able to demonstrate all the contexts of the underlying case from his position and deliver the respective technical and economic data.

Of course, the decision maker will – if he does not already possess enough knowledge on the subject in question himself – get this information from his staff or other competent sources. To see the full picture, however, it is important for him to also consider the arguments of the concerned stakeholders. In that sense, the lobbyist can be really helpful. But he must also be aware, at all times, that he can only deliver the data, since the decision maker can choose when and from whom he wants information.

It is needless to say that successful lobbying is based on honesty. The lobbyist has to put his cards on the table and also declare his absolute limits, i.e. the potential regulation he would, in the worst case, be able to live with. This includes taking an honest position regarding the technical possibilities of alternative solutions – even if they do not fit into the lobbyist's or his stakeholder's business strategy. Otherwise, lobbying can backfire.

This is best illustrated by a few examples culled from my own 28 years of experience in different parliaments:

Regarding a law on limits for car emissions, some car manufacturers sadly told the Parliament that, unfortunately, most of what the Parliament wanted to achieve was not feasible technically. After this became public, engineers from companies that felt offended in their professionalism called Members of Parliament anonymously to tell them that they would certainly be able to technically solve the problem, if one would only let them do so. Well, those car manufacturers did not do themselves a favor.

Also, one should avoid raising different demands with different decision makers. When talking to Members of Parliament from a party generally regarded as "more business friendly", a lobbyist should not ask them to push for a certain, less restrictive legislative solution, saying that otherwise it would be the end of this whole sector of economy – while telling another party that one could well live with the planned regulation as long as it would not become more severe. With such double standards a lobbyist loses all credibility.

Another important issue for good lobbying is personal knowledge of the decision makers and respective conversation on the matters in question. It's needless to say that hectographed letters claiming that one expects(!) Members of Parliament to negatively vote on Articles x and y in a certain legislative draft, without even explaning why, immediately find their way to the dustbin. Yes, those things do happen. The same applies for ambush methods of contacting decision makers in the corridors immediately before a plenary or committee session. This is more than annoying and delivers the respective results. Even if "lobbying" does literally derive from informal meetings in Parliaments' lobbies and halls, nowadays more sophisticated methods than an uninvited and intrusive appeal should be used.

Which methods should be used, in what cases does lobbying make sense, when and where should it take place – all those questions are answered by this valuable, experience based lobbying handbook.

Prof. Dr. h. c. Siegbert Alber,
former Advocate General of
the European Court of Justice,
Vice President of the European
Parliament and Member of the
German Bundestag

Introduction

This is a how-to-do-it handbook about lobbying in the European Union. If you are a company CEO, association or NGO representative, or the one in charge of your company's government relations, public affairs or public policy affairs - this handbook aims to give you practical guidance when looking for an effective way to influence the European legislative and administrative bodies. Whether you represent a stakeholder from Europe, the US, Russia, China, India or elsewhere – the intention of this book is to help you find your way through the jungle of EU decision making.

How do I succeed in influencing the EU's legislative process? How do I influence EU politics and administrative decisions? When should I talk to whom about what? And whom do I have to invite for lunch for which purpose? Do I walk alone or do I need a consultant and who are my allies?

Though lobbying is not easy, it can be learned. This EU guide presents the players, the arena and the necessary strategies and techniques to deal with the EU. It shows the methods and tactics that EU lobbyists can use to take action regarding their concerns and problems. It equips you with the necessary tools for the lobbying process - from monitoring, to grass roots campaigning, to preparing your own legislative drafts.

This manual for EU lobbying shows you how to get your voice heard in the increasingly louder environment of EU politics, business and media - and how to get your arguments considered in a world of information overflow.

Andreas Geiger

Brussels, September 2006

I. What is lobbying?

Lobbying is the professional practice of advocating private and public interests towards legislators and decision makers. Its goal is to influence the governing bodies. The days when people in Europe thought of lobbying as something informal and somehow "dodgy", something that is practiced in a twilight zone and often enough involves bribery and other criminal acts, are over. Lobbyists are well-accepted stakeholders in the political decision making process of the EU since lobbying is an essential part of democracy. The Greek knew it and so did the Romans. The term "lobbying" in fact descends from the Latin word "lobia", meaning the galleries and halls of the Roman Senate where the exchange of political information took place.

With regard to modern democracies, lobbying was born in the USA as an extension of the rights deriving from the First Amendment of the US-Constitution. Some say it even dates back to the days of President Abraham Lincoln, when business stakeholders tried to influence Members of Congress in the lobby of the US Congress building. Others refer back to the time of the President Ulysses S. Grant administration, between 1869 and 1877. Not being allowed to smoke in the White House by his wife, Grant enjoyed his cigars in the lobby of the nearby Willard Hotel. Having been spotted there often, politicians and others wanting political favors began to accompany him during this time of repose, while he was in high spirits. Since then, lobbying in Washington, usually being referred to as "K Street", consistently grew as a political factor. As long ago as 1913, President Woodrow Wilson complained that Washington was „swarming with lobbyists (...) you can't throw a brick in any direction without hitting one".

In contrast, lobbying in Brussels was only born in the late 1970s. Up to that time, "diplomatic lobbying" at the highest levels remained the rule. There were few lobbyists involved in the system and, except for some business associations, representative offices were rarely used. The event that sparked the explosion of lobbying was the first direct election of the European Parliament in 1979. Up until then, the Parliament consisted of delegated members from the national parliaments. Through that change, EU decision making became more complex, and companies increasingly felt the need of an expert local presence to find out what was going on in Brussels. The cornerstone of lobbying was, therefore, the need to provide information. It then

Lobbying in Brussels was only born in the late 1970s

developed the need to influence the process actively and effectively[1]. The next important step in lobbying development was the Single European Act in 1986 which both created the qualified majority vote for taking decisions in the Council and enhanced the role of the Parliament, again making EU legislation more complex and lobbying more important and attractive for stakeholders. In brief, the stronger the EU developed from a Member States organisation to an active political player in the world, the more policy areas it covered, the more important it became as a lobbying target. With the EU enlargement in 2004 this development has taken a step further, bringing in not only a lot more players and stakeholders but also a wide range of different political cultures and traditions.

While on one hand this process and the latest lobbying scandals in the US and in some EU Member States have led the EU to push for stricter and more formalised lobbying rules[2], on the other the EU institutions have expressively acknowledged the described function of and the need for lobbying.

EU initiative on Lobbying

In its recent policy papers on more transparency in the EU, the European Commission states as follows[3]:

"(...) "lobbying" means all activities carried out with the objective of influencing the policy formulation and decision-making processes of the European institutions. Accordingly, "lobbyists" are defined as persons carrying out such activities, working in a variety of organisations such as public affairs consultancies, law firms, NGOs, think tanks, corporate lobby units ("in-house representatives") or trade associations. For a meaningful discussion on how to frame lobbying at EU level, it is necessary to define the basic framework on which the relationship between the EU institutions and lobbyists should be built. The Commission views the following components as essential:

1. Lobbying is a legitimate part of the democratic system, regardless of whether it is carried out by individual citizens or companies, civil society organisations and other interest groups or firms working on behalf of third parties (public affairs professionals, think tanks and lawyers).
2. Lobbyists can help bring important issues to the attention of the European institutions. In some cases, the Community offers financial support in order to ensure that views of certain interest groups are effectively voiced at European level (consumer interests, disabled citizens, environmental interests, etc.).

[1] Harris/Fleisher, The Handbook of Public Affairs, p. 51
[2] See chapter "How to lobby"
[3] Green Paper on European Transparency Initiative, p.5: http://ec.europa.eu/commission_barroso/kallas/doc/com2006_0194_4_en.pdf

3. At the same time, undue influence should not be exerted on the European institutions through improper lobbying.
4. When lobby groups seek to contribute to EU policy development, it must be clear to the general public which input they provide to the European institutions. It must also be clear who they represent, what their mission is and how they are funded.
5. Inherent in the European institutions' obligation to identify and safeguard the "general interest of the Community" is their right to hold internal deliberations without interference from outside interests.
6. Measures in the field of transparency must be effective and proportionate."

The reason for the acknowledgement of EU lobbying as a legitimate and necessary task is simple: all business activities of the corporate world are influenced by politics and the decisions and measures taken by governments. Tomorrow's law is therefore the basis for today's worldwide business strategies. Politicians cannot govern without regard to industry and other stakeholders. The growing complexity of economic structures overtaxes the legislators' resources more and more. Those involved in the legislative process in the EU are therefore – as their counterparts in the US have been doing for many years – increasingly turning to industry representatives, associations, NGOs, law and lobbying firms in order to obtain comprehensive information on technical, economic and legal issues before making a decision. This allows the stakeholders to provide constructive input in the political decision making process by giving the legislator the necessary information he needs for his decision. European lobbying is a reciprocal political consulting process in which legislator and stakeholders exchange information on the issue in question. Ideally, this process should result in avoiding subsequent legal problems of new legislation or decisions - which is far better for all sides than resolving legal disputes in court once legislation or decisions have been adopted. Lobbying, in its proper sense, means expressing the interests of stakeholders to political decision makers in an open political dialog with the legislative bodies. With one major goal: making the law better before-hand to avoid legal disputes afterwards. Otherwise, like in an ancient Greek tragedy, all characters may be right in their argumentative acting but, if unwilling to compromise, dead in the final act[4].

Lobbying is a legitimate and necessary task

Nowadays, professional lobbying is a high-end management discipline at the crossing point of politics, economy and society. And it is a booming market. It has both elements of legal counsel and

[4] van Schendelen, Machiavelli in Brussels, p. 47

PR, though being a field of its own. Legal counsel, due to its major task in influencing the legislator or decision maker so that the law is adapted to the stakeholder's arguments in the legislative process. PR, because this work needs proper communication to convince the legislator accordingly.

Lobbying is partly law, partly PR

Lobbying is generally referred to as the practice of "public affairs" or "government relations". This happens because lobbying involves the management of a stakeholder's affairs in society and public, hence the name "public affairs". This is part of its PR side. But hardcore lobbying has, in fact, a stronger focus on the legislative side, trying to influence the law and decision making process directly. Here, its focus is on keeping permanent relationships with governments and parliaments, therefore being known as "government relations". Having realised the importance of this key function, EU stakeholders tend to follow the US model, having lobbyists directly counsel their CEOs or chairmen, whether as an external consultant or in their corporate function as "Head of Government Relations". This follows the concept which has been applied already for legal issues with regard to external attorneys or internal General Counsels in companies in the past.

Due to globalisation, EU lobbying is increasingly becoming a part of worldwide lobbying strategies of the corporate world and of other stakeholders. Not only does industry need to have more or less the same legal framework for its market activity in all countries to save on production costs, but the legislators on the different continents also tend to copy each other's ideas on new policy frameworks. Consequently, lobbying has grown significantly, over the past decade, into one of the major areas of strategic management activity on a worldwide scale. EU lobbying has become a strategic core business function for companies and all other stakeholders that wish to compete successfully and operate internationally. EU lobbying is now at the cutting edge as an interpreter of complex governmental EU policies and respective stakeholder demands.

II. Who is lobbying?

When lobbying your interests in Brussels, you need to be aware of one important thing: you are not alone.

There are currently around 15,000 lobbyists in Brussels (consultants, lawyers, associations, corporations, NGOs, etc.) seeking to influence the EU's legislative process. Some 2,600 special interest groups have a permanent office in Brussels[5]. Their distribution is roughly as follows: European trade federations (32%), consultants (20%), companies (13%), NGOs (11%), national associations (10%), regional representations (6%), international organisations (5%) and think tanks (1%)[6]. And the number is increasing fast. The Washington Times put it this way: "There are not many growth industries in Brussels, the capital of Belgium and headquarters of the EU, but lobbying is definitely one of them".[7] So go ahead, take a shot. These are your fellow lobbyists:

There are currently around 15,000 lobbyists in Brussels

1. Companies

Almost all major corporations, the so-called "global players", have meanwhile set up representative offices in Brussels to cover their political issues: DaimlerChrysler, McDonalds', General Electric – to name a few. Today, they sum up to about 250 EU lobbying offices. 37 percent are US companies, 5 percent from Japan, 9 percent each from France and the UK and 7 percent from Germany[8]. The reason for this is twofold. First, lobbying is a long established business in Washington, so this is not new for US companies. And many US companies have recently realised – mainly due to some merger and cartel decisions of the Commission, like GE/Honeywell and Microsoft – that they could no longer "walk all over" Brussels and therefore decided to join the game. Secondly, historically speaking, the industry and trade associations covered most of the political interests of the corporate world in Europe. Only a few European companies like DaimlerChrysler have joined the political process in Brussels almost from the beginning. The majority of European companies made the decision to follow the Washington D.C. model of individual interest

[5] http://www.euractiv.com/Article?tcmuri=tcm:29-140650-16&type=LinksDossier; [6] van Schendelen, Machiavelli in Brussels, p. 46
[7] Harding, Analysis: Reining in EU Lobbyists, The Washington Times, 8 March 2005.; [8] Greenwood, Interest representation in the European Union, p. 122

representation only much later when they realised that being in the same industry or trade association with most of their largest competitors was not always helpful to really find one common position on all political issues. And if such position was found at all it would not cover all aspects of the companies' individual interests and problems on the subject. Furthermore, companies saw the rising importance of EU legislation and its implications on their daily business. Giving your company a face of its own in the political arena by putting your flag into Brussels ground was therefore a consequent decision for most of them.

While some larger companies have been present for a while, even the small and medium sized companies (SMEs), which do not constitute the basis of the large stock indexes like Dow Jones, DAX, CAC40, can now be found in the Brussels arena with their own people. SMEs are often underestimated in their lobbying power, but they provide for a large part of the EU's economy. In Germany, the largest EU economy, they make up for 99 percent of all enterprises and provide 70 percent of all employees. SMEs are also the ones most directly hit by new EU regulation since they have fewer possibilities of shifting their business to other sectors or countries. As a result, SMEs are especially in need of an effective interest representation in Brussels, which - mostly for monetary reasons - they had left to their respective industry associations in the past. But now this is changing.

Companies are increasingly setting up representative offices

The next wave of companies to cement their presence in Brussels in the coming decade will surely comprise large players from emerging world economies, such as China and India.

Most of the company representations are rather small, made up of two or three people, with anything over five being an exception. While some are staffed by senior personnel with support staff and a degree of autonomy, at the opposite end are those holding a relatively junior position within their company, working alone in Brussels with part-time secretarial assistance[9].

The advantage of being a company representative in the lobbying process is the fundamental technical expertise and business knowledge you can provide to the EU institutions. Companies are directly active in the market and are therefore particularly good and well accepted at providing expert knowledge to the EU. To the extent that different parties, i.e. workers, managers and shareholders, are involved in the formulation of a firm's interest, companies can also provide important national Member State information, which might differ from the official information the Member State provides. This is what makes them interesting for the EU institutions. The hierarchical decision making structure within companies also guarantees the efficient provision of information to the EU institutions.

If you are a company, your business strategy can be regional, national or European. However, for most of the firms it is difficult to claim to provide truly European or public information since only the individual firm is involved in the articulation of the interest[10]. This is your major disadvantage as a company representative: whether large or small, you only speak for yourself.

2. Associations

There are associations for almost everything in Brussels: European associations, international associations, national associations, regional associations, local associations. There are industrial associations, professional associations, trade associations, umbrella associations. Associations whose members are corporations and associations whose members are other associations. Around 950 formally constituted associations are organised and operated at the EU level[11]. Certainly, they can only coexist because most of them are highly specialised. Whilst many specialisations can be explained around divisions in the product chain, clustered around upstream extractors of raw materials and downstream enterprises bringing products to the market, others reflect issues rather than sectoral clusters. For instance, the Alliance for Beverage Cartons and the Environment (ACE) is a highly specific association representing the interests of carton and beverage container manufacturers, such as Tetra-Pak, in environmental policy-making. Others represent issues across sectors, such as the European Brands Association representing the interests of manufacturers of most proprietary products (washing powders, designer labels etc.) with regard to generics.

Around 950 associations operate in Brussels

One of the most influential associations is probably the Union des Industries de la Communauté Européenne (UNICE), which represents industry interests and in 2006 was composed of 39 national federations from 33 countries. Its Brussels headquarters has around 45 staff members. It coordinates seven policy committees and 60 working groups summing up to 1,200 experts, and prepares about 100 position papers a year for the EU institutions[12]. UNICE's counterpart, the European Trade Union Confederation (ETUC) defends the interests of

---

[10] Bouwen, A comparative study of business lobbying in the European Parliament, the European Commission and the Council of Ministers, p. 11
[11] Greenwood, Interest representation in the European Union, p. 75
[12] http://www.unice.org/content/Default.asp?PageID=212

60 million workers and labor unionists. It comprises 76 member organisations from a total of 40 countries and 11 industry federations.

The American Chamber of Commerce to the European Union (AmCham EU) promotes the interests of around 135 European companies of American parentage that have manufacturing plants throughout the EU. Each member company has representatives on AmCham EU and takes part in the activities of the 14 committees, two task forces and several working groups. Other important interest groups include the European Round Table of Industrialists (ERT), which gathers around 45 chief executive officers from Europe's largest companies, the Union Européenne de l'Artisanat et des Petites et Moyennes Entreprises (UEAPME) and the Fédération Bancaire de l'Union Européenne (FBE), which represents over 4,500 European banks from 27 national banking associations. EUROCHAMBRES (The Association of European Chambers of Commerce and Industry), on the contrary, represents 44 national associations of Chambers of Commerce and Industry, that is to say, a European network of 2,000 regional and local Chambers with over 18 million member enterprises in Europe[13].

The general advantage of being an association in the lobbying process is the sheer mass of stakeholders, which you usually represent, speaking for a whole sector or even for a whole industry. Your major problem is that most of your members are directly competing companies in the market, giving you a hard time in articulating policy positions that fit all of their interests. Associations are usually not as good as individual firms at providing detailed expert knowledge, mostly due to the fewer resources they have and the wider range of issues they deal with. But they are well accepted by the EU institutions[12] for the provision of more general policy information. Because of their multi-layered organisational structure, associations are often too distant from the direct market problems and, therefore, they

The national associations often are also umbrella associations, having other national or local associations as their members mostly have to rely on their members' information. The European associations' three-layer structure (EU level, national level, company level) also hampers the efficient provision of hardcore information. European associations are specialised in building consensus positions by channeling the different opinions of their member associations. They aggregate the interests of their member associations that are already the result of a bundling of needs and interests of these national associations' member companies. This extensive consultation mechanism allows the European associations to present an encompassing European perspective on their sector and thereby to provide good quality European information. However, the internal decision making processes for building consensus are complex, and negatively affect the efficient provision of information. A similar reasoning can be applied to national associations. They represent the national sectoral interest and therefore are accepted for providing high-quality national market information[14].

The reason for belonging to an association, or at least for being active in one is, as mentioned before, that the more stakeholders you have behind you, the more likely you gain access to the EU institutions. However, since a common approach is not always possible due to the diverging opinions of the association members on EU subjects and policies, not only do most companies, as described above, have an EU office of their own, but so do most of the national associations that are members of a European association. One example is the Federation of German Industries (BDI), a cross-sector association representing large parts of the German industry landscape. Although having a Brussels office of its own and being a well-recognised player in Brussels, the BDI is also a member of UNICE. The same model applies for sector associations. For example, most of the national banking federations from the Member States also have their own EU office in Brussels, but of course, it is also they who constitute the membership basis for the European Banking Federation (FBE). National associations often are umbrella associations themselves, having other national or local associations as their members, whom again create their membership from the Member State's companies. Again, taking the BDI as an example, one of its members is the German Association of the Automotive Industry (VDA), amongst whose members are German car manufacturers like DaimlerChrysler and BMW. Picking up the banking sector example from above, one of the members of the European Banking Federation (FBE) is the Association of German Banks (BDB) amongst whose members are Deutsche Bank and Commerzbank.

While large national umbrella associations like the ones mentioned have such a national political weight that their future Brussels existence is beyond doubt, the smaller associations have a more difficult time to find their place on the EU level. Many of them find themselves in the position of "sandwich lobbyists" being jammed in between their member companies' lobbyists and their European umbrella organisations' lobbyists, to a certain extent lacking the Brussels use and legitimacy they still have on the national level.

---

[14] Bouwen, A comparative study of business lobbying in the European Parliament, the European Commission and the Council of Ministers, p. 11

3. NGOs

Being an NGO can be fun since you will enjoy the fact that the EU institutions regard you as a necessary counterweight to industry lobbying. You are representing the public good. Right or wrong, whose information about fauna and flora protection will be regarded more critically by the EU legislator: the one provided by WWF and Greenpeace – or the one provided by multinational companies like Shell or BP planning a new oil platform?

Environment, human rights, gender equality, health sector, education, and social welfare – the most well-known and influential NGOs are probably: Greenpeace, Amnesty International and World Wide Fund for Nature (WWF)

Among the top issues of non-governmental organisations (NGOs) are environment, conservation and ecology, labour conditions and human rights, trade policies, wages and working conditions, education, health and social welfare[15]. The most well known and influential are probably Greenpeace, Amnesty International, Transparency International and World Wide Fund for Nature (WWF). Consumer organisations like the Association of European Consumers (AEC) or social NGOs like the Red Cross complete the range of NGOs.

Usually, NGOs are equipped to engage EU policy-making at a technical level, through permanent resources and supporting scientists. And they have the ability to turn science into politics through their mass mobilisation base when required. Besides providing technical expertise in the EU legislative process, NGOs also make particular use of campaigning instruments and mass media PR in their political lobbying. Many of the issues they fight for have an emotional aspect, which makes it easy for them to reach people. Whether it is about cutting down tropical rain forests or slaughtering baby seals – by creating public pressure an NGO will often get its arguments through a lot easier than by sticking to legal arguments only.

Since especially most Southern and Eastern European Member States have strong religious traditions, the church is also an important player in the EU lobbying market. Many of the various EU churches both have a representative office of their own in Brussels and are represented in The Conference of European Churches (CEC), which is a fellowship of 126 Orthodox, Protestant, and Old Catholic Churches, along with 43 associated organisations in Europe.

Other important NGOs active in the market include the so-called political party foundations and think tank interest groups. Among those study and research centres that aim to influence thinking among EU policy-makers, the main representatives are the European Policy Centre (EPC), the Centre for European Policy Studies (CEPS) and the Friends of Europe. However, those institutions are still few in number and far from reaching the amount of political influence in Brussels as their counterparts do in Washington.

4. Governments

Governments are not only lobbying targets at home. They are also active lobbyists on other political playgrounds themselves. Therefore, different national and local governments lobbying the EU legislators, with their respective interests, are important Brussels players.

Regarding the Member States, this kind of lobbying happens primarily through the Member States representatives in the Council, as described later on[16]. It also happens through the Permanent Representations of the Member States, which are home to their ambassadors to the EU.

In addition, Brussels hosts many third country delegations, which, through their Embassies and Missions, lobby for their national interest at the EU institutions. This is not only the case for such obvious political players like the US or Russia but also for many Third World countries. One major issue in the future will probably be the lobbying by African governments both for development aid and for opening the EU market with regard to their natural resources.

Embassies and Missions play an important role

However, EU institutions are not only lobbied by national government representatives. The sub-national level also plays an important role. This form of lobbying takes place mainly through the offices of Member States' local authorities. On one hand, their interests are promoted by the Council of European Municipalities and Regions (CEMR) and by the Assembly of European Regions (AER). On the other hand, since the EU's competences have increased over time and the impact of EU legislation on regional issues have become stronger, the different regions in the Member States influence European legislation themselves in those policy areas where they have legislative powers within their own Member State. They want to be present in order to provide their home institutions in the Member States (regional authorities, ministries, etc.) with information about upcoming legislation. The second objective is to organise and participate in events such as seminars and conferences in order to promote themselves and their territories, to attract investment, and to look for regional partnerships. The nearly 170 EU offices of the regions embrace considerable diversity. Some are Federal ministries staffed by civil servants,

[16] See chapter "Who is lobbied?"

while others are regional, city or local authorities or their national associations. Regional and sub-regional alliances, including cross-border regional alliances are included in this number. The activity and size of those offices depend on the region's degree of autonomy. Office size therefore varies from the Bavarian office housed in a chateau style building employing around 17 executive staff members to outsourced arrangements where a single consultant undertakes all the work on behalf of a number of territorial entities.[17]

5. Lobbying firms, law firms, PR firm and consultancies

Another way through which you can lobby the EU is by resorting to third parties, such as consultants specialised in EU matters. The number of consultancies dealing with EU affairs aimed at assisting companies or associations saw a sharp increase in the last few years. The expansion of direct lobbying in Brussels through consultancies is still an ongoing process. Whether they now claim to provide for lobbying, government relations or public affairs services, in the past they used to only inform and consult you about ongoing EU legislation, leaving the hardcore lobbying work to you. Recently, they began to increase their scope – by talking not only to you but also in the other direction: to the legislator. However, the quality and extent of these consulting services generally still fall behind what law firms and lobbying firms provide for in Washington.

Washington style pure lobbying firms – comparable to Dutko, Van Scoyoc or Carmen Group - have not been part of the Brussels lobbying scene so far. EU consultants either branded themselves as law firms, PR firms, think tanks or just "consultancies", mostly being frightened of the "lobbyist" image. This market perception has changed only recently. A comparable lobbying firm scene in Brussels, as it exists in Washington, can therefore be expected in the future. As a consequence, some of the Washington lobbying firms are also now expected to make a move to Brussels.

The relevance of law firms in the lobbying business is mainly due to both the role that European law plays in issues such as competition or business activity and to the precedence that it enjoys over national legislation. As a law firm, you have the advantage of being on a level playing field with the EU legislator. Furthermore, law firms mostly provide for one-stop-shopping since they are able to take the issue to the European Court of Justice if their lobbying fails. However, not many law firms have entered this business yet, usually claiming the allegedly "dodgy" character of lobbying, but in reality just lacking the right "political" personnel to do so. The few who have established themselves in this sector are either specialised boutique law firms like Alber & Geiger or large US law firms with a respective Washington lobbying practice expanding their scope to Brussels now. Those include firms like Hogan & Hartson, Mayer Brown, Wilmer Hale or Akin Gump.

In the past, PR or public affairs consultancies in Brussels usually focused on information gathering and monitoring services, mainly employing people with a non-legal background. Most consultancies attempt to change this now and spread their services into direct lobbying. Corporations or associations usually use the relatively non-expensive monitoring services provided by consultancies as a complementary instrument and a tool for further interest representation. This is even more important if you take into consideration the companies which do not possess the necessary resources on their own or that, for other reasons, decide not to open a liaison office in Brussels. For those companies, consultancies may constitute the only reliable source of on-the-ground services. This market is dominated by both the public affairs units of international public relations firms like APCO, Hill & Knowlton, Fleishman-Hillard or Burson-Marsteller and small, specialised consultancies like GPlus and others.

The EU institutions' acceptance of information that those "hired guns" deliver, depends largely on two factors: on the personal reputation of the individual lobbyists and on the clients they represent. Whoever pays the piper calls the tune. Usually, "hired guns" have therefore less acceptance speaking for European or national interests than the aforementioned players. They can, however, provide expert knowledge that often goes beyond the competencies of a single company or sector. When regulating a new policy field, the EU institutions usually refer to practices and laws from comparable fields (telecoms regulation – energy regulation; environment – consumer protection). From the experience they attained from working with their clients, consultants usually have a broad overview on subject matters and also on similar EU policy developments from other sectors where they have acted for their clients. Knowledge from other areas can then serve as a guideline for the new policy developments and proposals.

A consultant also has the advantage of being an "outsider". He is less likely to fall into the "personal-issues" trap, which can eas-

Tip

When looking for a consultant to help you with your lobbying efforts, have a checklist ready and compare several offers:

How long has the consultant been in the market?

What professional background do he and his team possess and does that help you with your problem?

What client references does he have?

ily happen to someone being an integral part of a stakeholder, e.g. a company representative or NGO staff member. Being overly involved in a particular issue of the stakeholder often leads to a lack of objectivity, lack of role clarity, and burnout. Beside the diversity of experience, an "outsider" will usually have a more distant view, fresh outlook, creative ideas and a more realistic perspective of what can be achieved[18] .

[18] Staples, Roots to power, p. 39

III. Who is lobbied?

The EU is one of the major political players in the world. Even though the EU is only about 40 percent the size of the US, its population is more than double the size. In fact, the EU population is the world's third largest after China and India[19].

COUNTRY	Surface area (millions km²)
China	9.6
EU	3.9
India	3.3
Japan	0.4
Russia	17.1
US	9.6

Surface area in millions of square kilometers

COUNTRY	Population in millions of people
China	1288.4
India	1064.4
EU	456.8
Japan	127.2
Russia	143.4
US	291.0

Population in millions of people

The EU is also a major world trading power. It accounts for approximately 20 percent of global imports and exports. The EU's gross domestic product (GDP) is about the same as that of the US.

COUNTRY	GDP (in billions Euro)
China	1253.0
EU	9755.4
Japan	3798.5
Russia	385.3
US	9727.7

GDP in billions Euro[20]

[19] http://europa.eu/abc/keyfigures/index_accessible_en.htm
[20] In 2003, http://europa.eu/abc/keyfigures/index_accessible_en.htm

Still, the US is the EU's biggest export market, and most of the goods entering the EU come from the US. But in the last years the EU's trade with China has also more than doubled in value, and China is now the second biggest supplier of EU imports. The EU's links to neighbouring Russia are also becoming consistently closer. Furthermore, the EU is a major importer of agricultural goods from developing countries. And finally, internal trade among the Member States themselves makes up for two thirds of all EU trade and accounts for over half of all trade in each Member State. In some cases, it amounts to around 80 percent.

Therefore, no matter whether you are a stakeholder from inside or outside the EU, you need to lobby the European Union. But, if you want to influence politics in the EU, you have to deal with the right decision makers. Therefore, as a lobbyist you need to know whom to lobby. This is determined by the way the relevant EU institutions are functioning and organised. In other words: Who does what and has which competencies?

There are several EU institutions. And as for their location in Brussels, they are all part of the "Quartier Europeén", a few blocks of Belgian soil concentrating almost the whole power of the EU.[21]

A virtual tour through the lobbying scene, including pictures of the relevant buildings is available on www.corporateeurope.org.

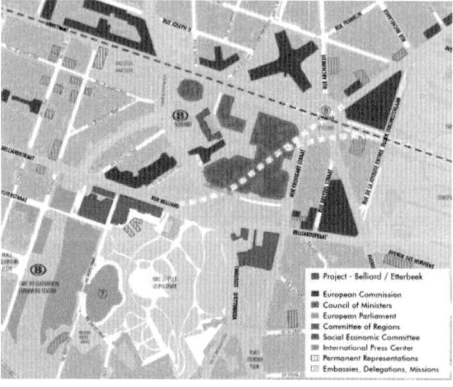

You can spend a lot of time trying to influence them. But since your resources are limited and decision making in the EU really involves only a few major players, you should stick to the following:

1. The European Commission

The Commission is probably the EU institution a lobbyist has to deal with the most - for its double function: legislative and administrative. The Commission not only drafts the proposals for new European laws (defined in Art. 249 EC) which it then presents to the Parliament and the Council. It is also the EU's executive arm – in other words, it is responsible for implementing the decisions of the Parliament and the Council. That means managing the day-to-day business of the EU: implementing its policies, running its programmes and spending its funds.

The Commission consists of one member from each Member State and is appointed every five years, within six months of the elections to the Parliament. The procedure is as follows:

The Commission has a double function: legislative and administrative

- The Member State governments agree jointly on whom to designate as the new Commission President.
- The Commission President-designate is then approved by the Parliament.
- The Commission President-designate, in discussion with the Member State governments, chooses the other members of the Commission.
- The new Parliament then interviews each Commission member and gives its opinion on the Commission team. Once it is approved, the new Commission can officially start to work.

The Commission remains politically accountable to the Parliament, which has the power to dismiss the whole Commission by adopting a motion of censure. Individual members of the Commission must resign if asked to do so by the President, provided the other Commissioners approve. It is up to the Commission President to decide which Commissioner will be responsible for which policy area, and to reshuffle these responsibilities if necessary during the Commission's term of office[23].

The Commission meets once a week, usually on Wednesdays in Brussels. The Commissioner responsible for the policy area in question presents each item on the agenda, and the whole team then takes a collective decision on it. The Commission attends all the sessions of Parliament, where it must clarify and justify its policies. It also replies regularly to written and oral questions posed by Members of the European Parliament (MEPs).

---

[23] Office for Official Publications of the European Communities, How the European Union works, p. 21

Chart
Commission[22]

 José Manuel Barroso

President

 Margot Wallström

:: Vice President
Institutional Relations
and Communication
Strategy

 Günter Verheugen

— Vice President
Enterprise and Industry

 Jacques Barrot

‖ ‖ Vice President
Transport

 Siim Kallas

— Vice President
Administrative Affairs,
Audit and Anti-Fraud

 Franco Frattini

‖ ‖ Vice President
Justice, Freedom and
Security

 Viviane Reding

=
Information Society and
Media

 Stavros Dimas

Environment

 Joaquin Almunia

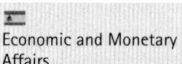
Economic and Monetary
Affairs

 Danuta Hübner

—
Regional Policy

 Joe Borg

Fisheries and Maritime
Affairs

 Dalia Grybauskaite

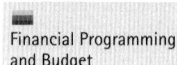
Financial Programming
and Budget

 Janez Potočnik

Science and Research

[22] http://ec.europa.eu/commission_barroso/index_en.htm

Ján Figel

Education, Training, Culture and Multilingualism

 Markos Kyprianou

Health and Consumer Protection

 Olli Rehn

Enlargement

 Louis Michel

Institutional Relations and Communication Strategy

 László Kovács

Taxation and Customs Union

 Neelie Kroes

Competition

 **Mariann Fischer Boel**

Agriculture and Rural Development

 Benita Ferrero-Waldner

External Relations and European Neighbourhood Policy

 Charlie McCreevy

Internal Market and Services

 Vladimir Špidla

Employment, Social Affairs and Equal Opportunities

 Peter Mandelson

Trade

 Andris Piebalgs

Energy

When you look at it from a lobbyist's point of view, the Commission is an ordinary bureaucracy with two exceptions. The first exception is its multicultural composition. The Commission reflects the variety of the EU. At all levels, from Commissioner to technical assistant, people have different languages, customs, values and norms. This variety far exceeds that of the national bureaucracy of a federal country like Germany or Spain. The Commission is also an example of multicultural integration, stimulated by such factors as a common location, the pragmatic use of only a few working languages (English, French and German) and shared expectations. It has a developing esprit de corps, although many cultural differences continue to play a role. The second exception regards the under-resourced nature of the Commission. Its total budget is almost equal to that of the Belgian federal government. Its administrative staff is only 2 percent of the size of the US federal government. The staff are about 30 percent secretarial (so-called C level), 10 percent linguistic (LA level), 5 percent technical (D level) leaving about 55 percent of the staff (about 10,500 persons) for policy work (A and B level)[24]. This is why the Commission is very dependent on outside support and information from lobbyists.

Also important when lobbying the Commission: it has different layers. A Commissioner has to run a portfolio, which seldom coincides with a Directorate General (DG), which is the technical term for the commission's departments. Most Commissioners have their feet in more than one DG and most DGs have more than one Commissioner. The Director General has to, therefore, maintain the order inside the DG since every DG consists of several Directorates and these have their specialised units. As a lobbyist you should be aware that as in any bureaucracy the substance of policy work is done at the mid-level. Most important are therefore the "chef de dossier" or the "case handler" respectively, and the Head of Unit above this person. They produce the draft papers for their superiors who normally only make comments or – if interested in the policy subject – have issued an instruction beforehand. In practice, the mass of policy papers moves like an iceberg through the Commission: only its small top is in the hands of the upper level civil servants and the Commissioners.

You should also be aware that every DG has its own set of policy tasks and structures to realise them - but the administrative segmentation does not fall in line with that of the policy fields. For example, the harmonisation of working times for truck drivers falls under DG Transport but is also an issue for DG Social Affairs, DG Internal Market, DG Enterprise, etc. The result is that the DG that is formally in charge tries to keep the lead while the others try to intervene at the earliest phase possible[25]. Regarding a certain policy issue, as a lobbyist you therefore have to keep in mind the different interests within the Commission itself – and use them. Getting your interests implemented in the EU's political process not necessarily always works best when taking the direct avenue. Sometimes you better play the puck against the boards.

Now, what roles and functions does the Commission have?

1.1 Legislation

The Commission has the "right of initiative".[26] In other words, the Commission alone is responsible for drawing up proposals for new EU legislation, which it presents to the Parliament and the Council. The Commission's staff is organised in departments, known as Directorates General (DGs) - as already mentioned above - and services (such as the Legal Service). Those administrative officials, experts, translators, interpreters and the secretarial staff do the day-to-day running of the Commission. There are approximately 25,000 European civil servants. Each DG is responsible for a particular policy area and is headed by a Director General who is accountable to one of the Commissioners. Overall coordination is provided by the Secretariat General, which also manages the weekly Commission meetings. The Secretariat is headed by the Secretary General, who is accountable directly to the President.

The Commission alone drafts the new laws

1.2 Administration

The Commission also has to manage the EU policies adopted by the Parliament and the Council, such as the common agricultural policy. Another example is competition policy, where the Commission has the power to authorise or prohibit mergers between companies.

The Commission further has to make sure that Member States do not subsidise their industries with state aids in such a way as to distort competition. For a lobbyist this function of the Commission is equally important as its legislative function. Here he can influence the way an adopted law is being administrated in practice. Further, more and more lobbying matters – like in competition law – are of

[25] van Schendelen, Machiavelli in Brussels, p. 65
[26] Office for Official Publications of the European Communities, How the European Union works, p.21

European Commission	Chief Economist	Director General
Directorate-General for Competition	D. NEVEN	Philip LOWE

Chart DG Competition[27]

| | | | Deputy Director-General MERGERS N. CALVIÑO | |

R	A	B	C	D
Strategic Planning and Resources Director: ... Adviser: J. RIVIERE YMARTI	**Policy and Strategic Support** Director: E. PAULIS	**Energy, Basic industries, Chemicals and Pharmaceuticals** Director: H. UNGERER	**Information, Communication and Media** Director: A. TRADACETE Adviser: C. RAKOVSKY	**Services** Director: C. MADERO Adviser: F. LOMHOLT

R-1	A-1	B-1	C-1	D-1
Strategic planning, human and financial resources, security M. MAGNIER	Antitrust policy and Scrutiny J. STRAGIER	Energy, Water L. KJOLBYE	Telecommunications and post; information society coordination M. ALBERS	Financial services (banking and insurance) I. SCHWIMANN

R-2	A-2	B-2	C-2	D-2
Information technology M. PEREZ ESPIN	Merger policy and Scrutiny C. ESTEVA MOSSO	Basic industries, Chemicals and Pharmaceuticals G. DE BRONETT	Media A. VANNINI	Transport L. MC CALLUM

R-3	A-3	B-3	C-3	D-3
Document management, information and communication C. DUSSART-LEFRET	European Competition Network and Institutional Relations K. DEKEYSER	Mergers I D. SJOBLOM	Information industries, Internet and consumer electronics ...	Distributive trades & other services Z. JAMBOR

A-4	B-4	C-4	D-4
International Relations B. RODRIGUEZ GALINDO	Mergers II ...	Mergers D. KLEEMANN	Mergers J. LUECKING

[27] http://ec.europa.eu/comm/dgs/competition/directory/organi_en.pdf

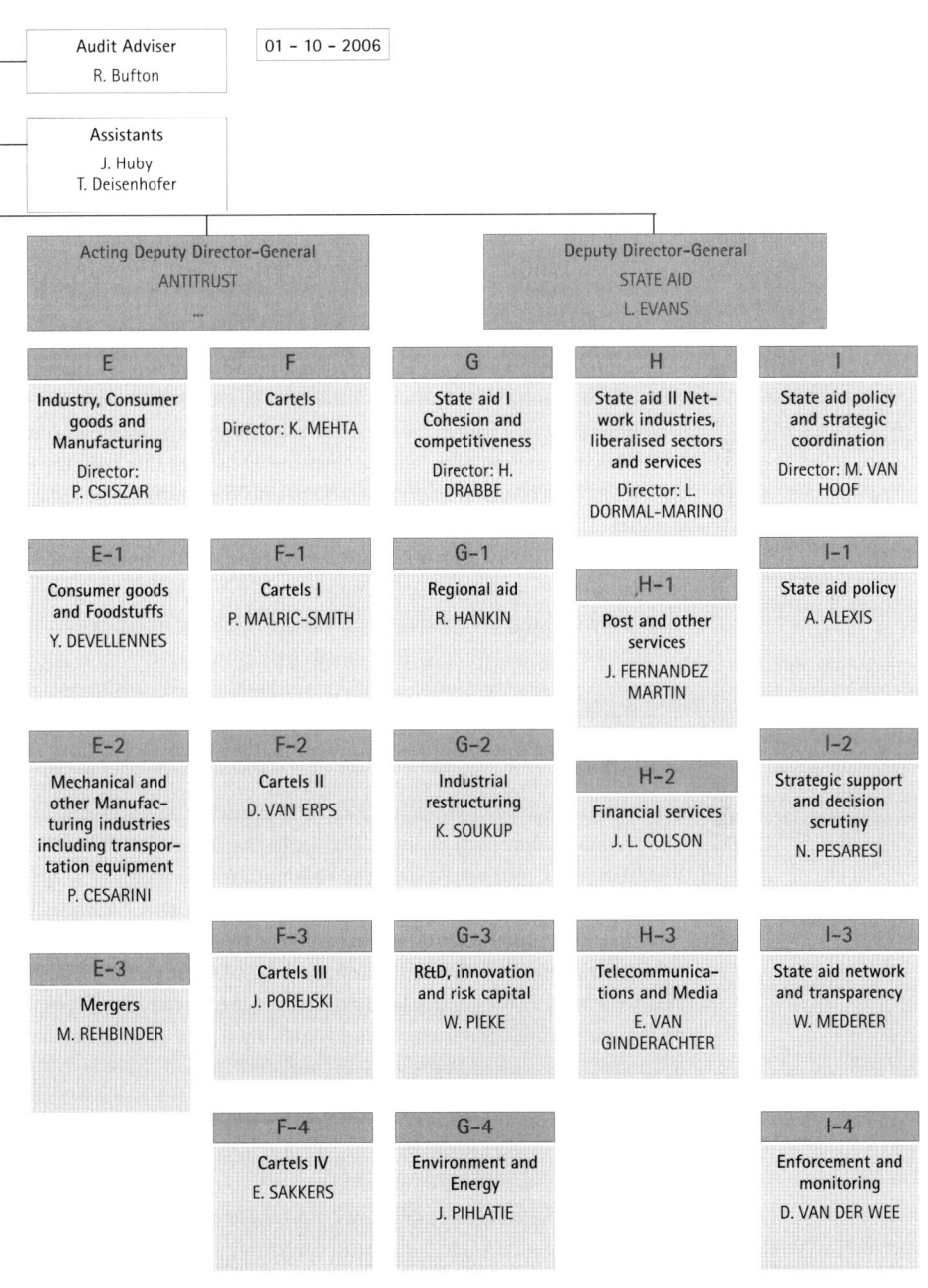

Audit Adviser
R. Bufton

01 - 10 - 2006

Assistants
J. Huby
T. Deisenhofer

Acting Deputy Director-General
ANTITRUST
...

Deputy Director-General
STATE AID
L. EVANS

E	F	G	H	I
Industry, Consumer goods and Manufacturing	Cartels	State aid I Cohesion and competitiveness	State aid II Network industries, liberalised sectors and services	State aid policy and strategic coordination
Director: P. CSISZAR	Director: K. MEHTA	Director: H. DRABBE	Director: L. DORMAL-MARINO	Director: M. VAN HOOF

E-1
Consumer goods and Foodstuffs
Y. DEVELLENNES

F-1
Cartels I
P. MALRIC-SMITH

G-1
Regional aid
R. HANKIN

H-1
Post and other services
J. FERNANDEZ MARTIN

I-1
State aid policy
A. ALEXIS

E-2
Mechanical and other Manufacturing industries including transportation equipment
P. CESARINI

F-2
Cartels II
D. VAN ERPS

G-2
Industrial restructuring
K. SOUKUP

H-2
Financial services
J. L. COLSON

I-2
Strategic support and decision scrutiny
N. PESARESI

E-3
Mergers
M. REHBINDER

F-3
Cartels III
J. POREJSKI

G-3
R&D, innovation and risk capital
W. PIEKE

H-3
Telecommunications and Media
E. VAN GINDERACHTER

I-3
State aid network and transparency
W. MEDERER

F-4
Cartels IV
E. SAKKERS

G-4
Environment and Energy
J. PIHLATIE

I-4
Enforcement and monitoring
D. VAN DER WEE

administrative origin, not of legislative. One example are the merger control decisions of the Commission. An adequate communication of the legal and political arguments with the intention to convince the Commission as an administrative authority is therefore becoming another important task of EU lobbying.

The Commission acts as "guardian of the treaties". This means that the Commission, together with the European Court of Justice, is responsible for making sure EU law is properly applied in all the Member States. If it finds that an EU country is not applying an EU law, and therefore not meeting its legal obligations, the Commission takes steps to put the situation right. First it launches a process called "infringement procedure". This involves sending the government an official letter, saying why the Commission considers this country is infringing EU law and setting it a deadline for sending the Commission a detailed reply. If this procedure fails to put things right, the Commission can then refer the matter to the European Court of Justice, which has the power to impose penalties. The Court's judgements are binding on the Member States and the EU institutions.

The Commission has a major function in competition law issues

1.3 Representation

The Commission is an important actor for the EU on the international stage. It enables the Member States to speak with one voice in international forums such as the World Trade Organization (WTO). The Commission is also responsible for negotiating international agreements on behalf of the EU. One example is the Cotonou Agreement, which sets out the terms of an important aid and trade partnership between the EU and developing countries in Africa, the Caribbean and the Pacific. Since many lobbying efforts are directed to international trade issues, the Commission in its function as dialog partner of the WTO, is an important lobbying target.

1.4 Budget

As the EU's executive body, the Commission is further responsible for managing and implementing the EU budget, currently 116 billion Euro for the year 2006. Most of the actual spending is done by national and local authorities, but the Commission is responsible for supervising it - under the watchful eye of the Court of Auditors.

Both institutions aim to ensure good financial management. Only if it is satisfied with the Court of Auditors' annual report does the Parliament grant the Commission discharge for implementing the budget.[28]

2. The European Parliament

The Parliament is elected by the citizens of the EU to represent their interests. Elections are held every five years. The present Parliament has 732 members from 25 EU countries.

When lobbying the Parliament, you need to know that Members of the Parliament (MEPs) do not sit in national blocks, but in Europe-wide political groups. Between them, they represent all views on European integration, from pro-federalist to euro-sceptic. Those political parties are not in its basic sense working units. They are networks of so-called sister parties from the Member States.[29]

The Parliament has three places of work: Brussels, Luxembourg and Strasbourg. Luxembourg is home to the administrative offices, the General Secretariat. Only two of the three locations are of lobbying importance, since meetings of the whole Parliament, known as plenary sessions and committee meetings only take place in Strasbourg and Brussels.

To be able to lobby them accordingly you need to know how the parliamentary party groups divide themselves. The parties in the Parliament, in which conservatives, socialists, greens, liberals, etc. from the different Member States' parties try to find a common roof are shown below.

Numbers of seats per country

(in alphabetical order according to the country's name in its own language)

Country	Seats
Belgium	24
Czech Republic	24
Denmark	14
Germany	99
Estonia	6
Greece	24
Spain	54
France	78
Ireland	13
Italy	78
Cyprus	6
Latvia	9
Lithuania	13
Luxembourg	6
Hungary	24
Malta	5
Netherlands	27
Austria	18
Poland	54
Portugal	24
Slovenia	7
Slovakia	14
Finland	14
Sweden	19
United Kingdom	78
Total	732

[29] van Schendelen, Machiavelli in Brussels, p. 69

Parties in the Parliament

Group of the European People's Party (Christian Democrats) and European Democrats

Socialist Group in the European Parliament

Group of the Alliance of Liberals and Democrats for Europe

Group of the Greens / European Free Alliance

Confederal Group of the European United Left – Nordic Green Left

Independence / Democracy Group

Union for Europe of the Nations Group

Number of seats per political group, as at June 2, 2005

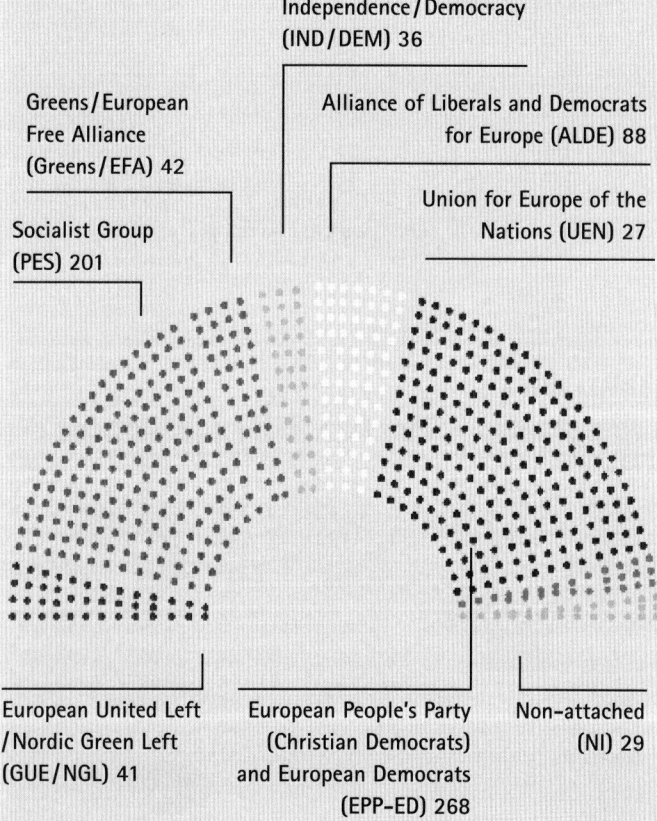

Independence / Democracy (IND / DEM) 36

Greens / European Free Alliance (Greens / EFA) 42

Alliance of Liberals and Democrats for Europe (ALDE) 88

Union for Europe of the Nations (UEN) 27

Socialist Group (PES) 201

European United Left / Nordic Green Left (GUE / NGL) 41

European People's Party (Christian Democrats) and European Democrats (EPP-ED) 268

Non-attached (NI) 29

The Parliament's work is divided into two stages:

- Preparing for the plenary session. This is done by the MEPs in the various parliamentary committees that specialise in particular areas of EU activity. The political groups also discuss the issues for debate.
- The plenary session itself. Plenary sessions are held in Strasbourg one week per month (from Monday to Thursday) and in between in Brussels (two-day sessions only). At these sessions, Parliament examines proposed legislation and votes on amendments before coming to a decision on the text as a whole.

The Parliament decides its annual calendar of work on the basis of a proposal by the Conference of Presidents. The calendar is divided into plenary sittings (part-sessions) and meetings. This calendar is your guideline if you want to lobby for the right issue at the right time in the right place. The calendar is structured into:

- 12 four-day part-sessions in Strasbourg and additional two-day part-sessions in Brussels,
- two weeks a month for meetings of parliamentary committees and interparliamentary delegations,
- one week a month for political group meetings
- four weeks a year where MEPs concentrate exclusively on constituency work.

Parliament's annual calendar 2007

The Parliament has three main functions[30]:

2.1 Legislation

The MEPs have a
permanentely increasing
importance

The Parliament has gained a lot of influence in the EU legislative process over the last decades and is therefore a major lobbying target nowadays. The most important legislative procedure for the Parliament, and at the same time the most common procedure for adopting EU legislation, is the so-called co-decision procedure[31] (Art. 251 EC) which places the Parliament and the Council on an equal footing. It applies to legislation in a wide range of fields. In some other fields (for example agriculture, economic policy, visas and immigration), the Council alone legislates, but it has to consult Parliament. In addition, Parliament's assent is required for certain important decisions, such as allowing new countries to join the EU. Parliament also provides impetus for new legislation by examining the Commission's annual work programme, considering what new laws would be appropriate and asking the Commission to put forward proposals. All this will be dealt with in more detail in following chapters.

The draft laws coming from the Commission are being discussed in and amendments are being made by the respective committee of the Parliament before the issue is taken to the plenum. A typical Parliament committee agenda is shown on the right.

You should know that for each respective EU policy area there is a committee in Parliament. In order to do the preparatory work for Parliament's plenary meetings, the MEPs are divided up among a number of specialised standing committees. A committee consists of between 25 and 78 MEPs (plus substitute members and observers from accession countries), and has a Chair, a bureau and a secretariat. The political make-up of the committees reflects that of the plenary assembly: the number of seats the various parties have in the committee roughly depends on their size in plenum. However, the size of the committees is still too large for effective action. To deal with the "corpulence", every major item on the agenda, such as a Commission proposal or a parliamentary initiative is given to a rapporteur. This MEP has the task of drafting a resolution acceptable to the majority of the committee and the plenum. It is a prestigious role, frequently given to the established MEPs of the larger parties. The rapporteur is closely watched by the so-called shadow rapporteurs from the other parties. To achieve an acceptable draft he has to anticipate many of the stakeholders' later

[30] Office for Official Publications of the European Communities, How the European Union works, p. 12.
[31] The different legislative procedures are being dealt with in detail later on.

EUROPEAN PARLIAMENT

ITRE (2006)0424_1

COMMITEE ON INDUSTRY, RESEARCH AND ENERGY

Meeting

Monday, 24 April 2006 from 15:00 to 18:30
Tuesday, 25 April 2006 from 9:00 to 12:30
Brussles

PUBLISHED DRAFT AGENDA

Monday, 24. April 2006, from 15:00 to 18:30 Brussles
1.   Adoption of draft agenda
2.   Announcements from the Chair
3.   Approval of minutes of meeting of
      Minutes of Extra meeting of 26/09/2005   PE362.850 v1–00
      Minutes of 22-23/11/05   PE365.089 v1–00
      Minutes of 24-26/01/06   PE368.001 v1–00
      Minutes of 20-21/02/06   PE370.185 v1–00

● ● ●

In the presence of the Council and the European Commission

4.   Research, technological development and demonstration activities
      (seventh framework programme, 2007-2013)
      ITRE/6/27693
                                                      PR - PE360.033 v1–00

Parliament
committee
agenda[32]

EUROPEAN PARLIAMENT

2004   2009

Commitee on Industry, Research and Energy

ITRE_PV(2005)0926_1

MINUTES
of the extraordinary meeting of Monday, 26 September 2005, from 18:30 to 20:00
STRASBOURG

The meeting opened at 18.36 on Monday 26 September 2005, with Giles Chichester (Chairman)
in the chair.

1.   **Adoption of draft agenda**
      The draft agenda was adopted in the form shown in these minutes.

2.   **Announcements from the Chair**
      Mr Seppänen report on "Supervision and control of shipments of radioactive waste
      and spent fuel" (COM(2004)0716 - 2004/0249 (CNS)) will not be voted on 5th
      October. A modified proposal from the Commission will be issued.

● ● ●

In the presence of the Council and the European Commission

VOTING TIME
3.   **Implementation of Protocol No 9 on the Bohunice V1 nuclear power plant in
      Slovakia**

Minutes
Parliament
committee
meeting[33]

The minutes of a
committee meeting,
showing the chairman
and rapporteur usually
look this way

---

[32] http://www.europarl.europa.eu/meetdocs/2004_2009/documents/oj/610/610080/610080en.pdf
[33] http://www.europarl.europa.eu/meetdocs/2004_2009/documents/pv/582/582062/582062en.pdf

demands[34]. Rapporteurs and shadow rapporteurs are the ones a lobbyist should target very closely as will be explained later.

The parliamentary committees meet once or twice a month in Brussels. Their debates are generally held in public. The committees draw up, may amend and adopt legislative proposals and own-initiative reports. They consider Commission and Council proposals and, where necessary, draw up reports to be presented to the plenary assembly. Parliament can also set up sub-committees and temporary committees to deal with specific issues, and committees of inquiry under its supervisory remit. The committee chairs coordinate the work of the committees in the Conference of Committee Chairmen.

You can look up all the actual Parliament committees and their current members on the respective Parliament website, so you know exactly whom to address[35]. The Parliament committees which also have their own websites[36], are listed in the table on the left.

2.2 Supervision

The Parliament exercises democratic supervision over the other European institutions. It does so in several ways. When a new Commission takes office, its members are nominated by the Member State governments but they cannot be appointed without the Parliament's approval. As explained above, the Parliament interviews each of them individually, including the prospective Commission President, and then votes on whether to approve the Commission as a whole. The Parliament also exercises control by regularly examining reports sent to it by the Commission (the annual general report, reports on the implementation of the budget, etc.). Moreover, MEPs regularly ask the Commission questions which the Commissioners are legally required to answer. The Parliament also monitors the work of the

Parliament Committees

AFET	Foreign Affairs
DEVE	Development
INTA	International Trade
BUDG	Budgets
CONT	Budgetary Control
ECON	Economic and Monetary Affairs
EMPL	Employment and Social Affairs
ENVI	Environment, Public Health and Food Safety
ITRE	Industry, Research and Energy
IMCO	Internal Market and Consumer Protection
TRAN	Transport and Tourism
REGI	Regional Development
AGRI	Agriculture and Rural Development
PECH	Fisheries
CULT	Culture and Education
JURI	Legal Affairs
LIBE	Civil Liberties, Justice and Home Affairs
AFCO	Constitutional Affairs
FEMM	Women's Rights and Gender Equality
PETI	Petitions
DROI	Human Rights
SEDE	Security and Defense
EQUI	Collapse of the Equitable Life Assurance Society
TDIP	Alleged use of European countries by the CIA for the transport and illegal detention of prisoners

[34] van Schendelen, Machiavelli in Brussels, p. 70
[35] http://www.europarl.europa.eu/activities/expert/committees.do?language=EN
[36] See for example for the Committee on Industry, Research and Energy: http://www.europarl.europa.eu/committees/itre_home_en.htm

Council. MEPs regularly ask the Council questions, and the President of the Council attends the Parliament's plenary sessions and takes part in important debates. The Parliament can exercise further democratic control by examining petitions from citizens and setting up inquiry committees.

Finally, the Parliament provides input to every EU summit (the European Council meetings). At the opening of each summit, the President of the Parliament is invited to express the Parliament's views and concerns about topical issues and the items on the Council's agenda.

2.3 Budget

The Parliament and the Council decide the EU's annual budget jointly. The Parliament debates the budget in two successive readings, and the budget does not come into force until the President of Parliament has signed it. Parliament's Committee on Budgetary Control (COCOBU) monitors how the budget is spent, and each year Parliament decides whether to approve the Commission's handling of the budget for the previous financial year. This approval process is technically known as granting discharge.

3. The Council of the European Union

The Council is the EU's main decision making body. The Presidency of the Council rotates every six months. In other words, each EU country in turn takes charge of the Council agenda and chairs all the meetings for a six-month period, promoting legislative and political decisions and brokering compromises between the Member States. The Presidency is assisted by the General Secretariat, which prepares and ensures the smooth functioning of the Council's work at all levels. A Deputy Secretary General in charge of managing the General Secretariat assists the Secretary General.

The Council has the final say

Furthermore, as mentioned in the beginning, each Member State has a Permanent Representation in Brussels that represents it and defends its national interest at EU level. The head of each representation is the country's ambassador to the EU. These ambassadors ("permanent representatives") meet weekly within the Permanent Representatives Committee (Coreper). The role of this committee is to prepare the work of the Council, with the exception of most agricultural issues, which are handled by the Special Committee on Agriculture. A number of working groups, made up of officials from the national administrations, assist Coreper.

Since the Council only meets a few times a year, the real Council work is done at the lower level of Coreper. If Coreper believes that the ministers can accept an issue for decision in the Council, it puts an "A" mark on that dossier. Such dossier, either single or brought together as a package, is rubberstamped at the next meeting of the Council. The others, the so called "B" dossiers, mostly remain undecided. The field work for that Coreper task is done by the about 300 working groups. Functionally, they can be compared with the committees in the Commission. They are representative experts doing the work. If they think a dossier is ready for decision they mark it with a roman "I" and send it to Coreper which makes the final check. The large majority of "A" dossiers for the Council's rubberstamping are "I" dossiers from the working groups. Compared to the Commission committees the Council working groups are however different in two respects. Firstly, they are less specialised. A working group also deals with related policy issues thus covering a broader policy area than a Commission committee does and being able to combine issues to some extent. Secondly, they are expected to consist of only nationally appointed administrative people. Most working group members have, indeed, an officially national government status, either as visitors from their ministry or as part of their national permanent representation in Brussels. But the growing practice is for both people from lobbying groups and regional representatives to appear as their national government representatives[37]. So there is an access point for lobbyists here, also.

When the Council meets, it represents the Member States, and therefore one minister attends its meetings from each of the EU's national governments. Which ministers attend which meeting depends on what subjects are on the agenda. If, for example, the Council is to discuss environmental issues, the Environment Minister will attend the meeting from each Member States' government and it will be known as the "Environment Council".

Altogether, there are nine different Council configurations[38].

- General Affairs and External Relations
- Economic and Financial Affairs (Ecofin)
- Justice and Home Affairs (JHA)
- Employment, Social Policy, Health and Consumer Affairs

[37] van Schendelen, Machiavelli in Brussels, p. 75
[38] Office for Official Publications of the European Communities, How the European Union works, p. 14

- Competitiveness
- Transport, Telecommunications and Energy
- Agriculture and Fisheries
- Environment
- Education, Youth and Culture

In practice, there are
different Councils

Decisions in the Council are taken by vote. The bigger the country's population, the more votes it has, but the numbers are weighted in favour of the less populous countries.

Germany, France, Italy and the United Kingdom	29
Spain and Poland	27
Netherlands	13
Belgium, Czech Republic, Greece, Hungary and Portugal	12
Austria and Sweden	10
Denmark, Ireland, Lithuania, Slovakia and Finland	7
Cyprus, Estonia, Latvia, Luxembourg and Slovenia	4
Malta	3
Total	321

Votes in
the council

In some particularly sensitive areas such as common foreign and security policy, taxation, asylum and immigration policy, Council decisions have to be unanimous. On most issues, however, the Council takes decisions by qualified majority voting (QMV). A qualified majority is reached

- if a majority of Member States (in some cases a two-thirds majority) approve and
- if a minimum of 232 votes is cast in favour – which is 72.3 % of the total.

In addition, a Member State may ask for confirmation that the votes in favour represent at least 62 % of the total population of the EU. If this is found not to be the case, the decision will not be adopted.
The Council has the following responsibilities[39]:

[39] Office for Official Publications of the European Communities, How the European Union works, p. 15.

3.1 Legislation

The Council and the Parliament adopt much EU legislation jointly, so the law cannot pass without being cleared by the Council. As mentioned, in some particularly sensitive areas such as taxation, Council decisions even have to be unanimous. In other words, each Member State has the power of veto in these areas. Those are the areas where a lobbyist can block a complete legislative proposal by just convincing one Member States' government to oppose the law in the Council.

3.2 Coordination

The Member States for example have decided that they want an overall economic policy based on close coordination between their national economic policies. The economics and finance ministers, who collectively form the Economic and Financial Affairs Council (Ecofin), carry out this coordination. The Member States also decided to create more jobs and to improve their education, health and social protection systems. Although each EU country is responsible for its own policy in these areas, they can agree on common goals and learn from each other's experience of what works best. This process is called the open method of coordination, and it takes place within the Council.

3.3 Third countries, outer and inner security

Security is only dealt with by the Council

There are areas of EU policy where a lobbyist doesn't even have a choice on whom to lobby since only the Council is in charge of that policy.

Each year the Council officially signs a number of agreements between the EU and non-EU countries, as well as with international organisations. These agreements may cover broad areas such as trade, cooperation and development or they may deal with specific subjects such as textiles, fisheries, science and technology, transport, etc. In addition, the Council may conclude conventions between the Member States in fields such as taxation, company law or consular protection. Conventions can also deal with cooperation on issues of freedom, security and justice. The Member States are further working to develop a common foreign and security policy (CFSP). However, foreign policy, security and defense are matters over which the individual national Member States governments retain independent control. They have not pooled their national sovereignty in these areas, so the Parliament and the Commission play only a limited role here. The Council is the main forum in which this intergovernmental cooperation takes place.

The same applies for inner security. To tackle cross-border crime requires cross-border cooperation between the national courts, police forces, customs officers and immigration services of all EU countries. The Justice and Home Affairs Council, i.e. the ministers for justice and of the interior, deal with such issues.

3.4 Budget

The Council and the Parliament decide the EU's annual budget jointly.

4. The European Court of Justice

Of course, you cannot lobby a court. The Court of Justice is not part of the legislative or administrative process of the EU. However, especially if you are a lawyer or focusing on legal lobbying arguments with the Commission, the Parliament and the Council, the Court of Justice can be of quite some use for you. Since none of the EU institutions is interested in creating bad laws, especially not illegal ones that in the end will fall in a court trial before the Court of Justice, they will surely listen to your legal arguments. In some cases probably even more than to your political ones. It therefore makes good sense to also focus your lobbying efforts on preventing such a situation for your stakeholder and the EU institutions. Both of them will welcome solving the potential legal dispute about a draft law during the drafting process instead of having a lengthy and costly court case afterwards accompanied by legal uncertainty in the meantime and a lot of public attention.

Tip
Use the Court of Justice as a lobbying tool when focusing on legal arguments in the legislative process

Also, if you fail in your lobbying efforts during the legislative or administrative process, you should consider continuing your efforts in the Court of Justice. In most cases of unsuccessful lobbying, you can forward the same legal arguments you made in the drafting process to the court case. In so far, the Court of Justice is even part of the game: if its decision is that the law or administrative decision at stake is null and void, the case is referred back to the hands of the legislative and administrative EU institutions whom you just lobbied - and the whole lobbying process starts again.

The Court of Justice is based in Luxembourg. Its job is to make sure that EU legislation is interpreted and applied in the same way in all Member States, so that the law is equal for everyone. It ensures, for example, that national courts do not give different rulings on the same issue. The Court of Justice also makes sure that Member States and institutions do what the law requires. It has the power to settle legal disputes between Member States, EU institutions, businesses and individuals[40].

The Court of Justice is composed of one judge per Member State, so that all 25 of the EU's national legal systems are represented. For the sake of efficiency, however, the Court of Justice rarely sits as a full court. It usually sits as a Grand Chamber of just 13 judges

Chambers of the Court of Justice[41]

FIRST CHAMBER
P. Jann, President of Chamber
R. Schintgen, A. Tizzano, A. Borg Barthet, M. Ilešič, E. Levits, JUDGES
SECOND CHAMBER
C.W.A. Timmermans, President of Chamber
P. Kūris, K. Schiemann, J. Makarczyk, L. Bay Larsen, J.C. Bonichot, JUDGES
THIRD CHAMBER
A. Rosas, President of Chamber
J. Klucka, J.N. Cunha Rodrigues, U. Lõhmus, A. Ó Caoimh, P. Lindh, JUDGES
FOURTH CHAMBER
K. Lenǎerts, President of Chamber
E. Juhász, R. Silva de Lapuerta, G. Arestis, J. Malenovský, T. von Danwitz, JUDGES
FIFTH CHAMBER
R. Schintgen, President of Chamber
A. Tizzano, A. Borg Barthet, M. Ilešič, E. Levits, JUDGES
SIXTH CHAMBER
P. Kūris, President of Chamber
K. Schiemann, J. Makarczyk, L. Bay Larsen, J.C. Bonichot, JUDGES
SEVENTH CHAMBER
J. Klucka, President of Chamber, President of Chamber
J.N. Cunha Rodrigues, U. Lõhmus, A. Ó Caoimh, P. Lindh, JUDGES
EIGHTH CHAMBER
E. Juhász, President of Chamber
R. Silva de Lapuerta, G. Arestis, J. Malenovský, T. von Danwitz, JUDGES

[40] Office for Official Publications of the European Communities, How the European Union works, p. 25.
[41] http://www.curia.eu.int/en/instit/presentationfr/composition/chambrescour.htm

or in chambers of five or three judges. The Court of Justice is assisted by eight Advocates General. Their role is to present reasoned opinions on the cases brought before the Court of Justice. They are all appointed to the Court of Justice by joint agreement between the governments of the Member States. Each is appointed for a term of six years, which may be renewed.

At the Court of Justice, the Court of First Instance is responsible for giving rulings on certain kinds of cases in first instance, particu-

CHAMBERS OF THE COURT OF FIRST INSTANCE	
FIRST CHAMBER	**EXTENDED COMPOSITION**
J. D. Cooke	B. Vesterdorf
R. García-Valdecasas	J. D. Cooke
I. Labucka	R. García-Valdecasas
M. Prek	I. Labucka
	M. Prek
SECOND CHAMBER	**EXTENDED COMPOSITION**
J. Pirrung	J. Pirrung
A. W. H. Meij	A. W. H. Meij
I. Pelikánová	N. J. Forwood
N. J. Forwood	I. Pelikánová
S. S. Papasavvas	S. S. Papasavvas
THIRD CHAMBER	**EXTENDED COMPOSITION**
M. Jaeger	M. Jaeger
V. Tiili	V. Tiili
J. Azizi	J. Azizi
E. Cremona	E. Cremona
O. Czúcz	O. Czúcz
FOURTH CHAMBER	**EXTENDED COMPOSITION**
H. Legal	H. Legal
V. Vadapalas	I. Wiszniewska–Bialecka
N. Wahl	V. Vadapalas
I. Wiszniewska–Bialecka	Moavero Milanesi
Moavero Milanesi	N. Wahl
FIFTH CHAMBER	**EXTENDED COMPOSITION**
M. Vilaras	M. Vilaras
M. E. Martins Ribeiro	M. E. Martins Ribeiro
F. Dehousse	F. Dehousse
D. Šváby	D. Šváby
K. Jürimäe	K. Jürimäe

Chambers of the
Court of First
Instance[42]

---

[42] http://www.curia.eu.int/en/instit/presentationfr/composition/chambrestribunal.htm

larly actions brought by private individuals, companies and some organisations, especially cases relating to competition law. The Court of
Justice and the Court of First Instance each have a President, chosen
by their fellow-judges to serve for a renewable term of three years.

Further, a European Civil Service Tribunal has been set up to adjudi-
cate in disputes between the EU and its civil service. This tribunal is composed of seven judges and is attached to the Court of First Instance.

If you need to take your lobbying case to court, you should know the
following: the Court of Justice gives rulings on cases brought before it.
Cases are submitted to the registry and a specific judge and Advocate
General are assigned to each case. The procedure that follows is in two
stages: first a written and then an oral phase. At the first stage, all the
parties involved submit written statements and the judge assigned to the
case draws up a report summarising these statements and the legal background for the case. Then comes the second stage - the public hearing.
Depending on the importance and complexity of the case, this hearing
can take place before a chamber of 3, 5 or 13 judges, or before the full
Court of Justice. At the hearing, the parties' lawyers put their case before
the judges and the Advocate General, who can question them. The Advocate General then gives his opinion, after which the judges deliberate and
deliver their judgment. Judgments of the Court of Justice are decided by
a majority and pronounced at a public hearing. There are no dissenting
opinions. Decisions are broadcasted on the day of delivery.

The four most common types of cases are:

4.1 The preliminary ruling procedure

The most important
Court proceedings

This is especially important if you want to challenge a national law
along the lines of EU law. The national courts in each EU country
are responsible for ensuring that EU law is properly applied in that
country. But there is a risk that courts in different countries might
interpret EU law in different ways. To prevent this from happening,
there is a preliminary ruling procedure (Art. 234 EC). This means that
if a national court has any doubt about the interpretation or validity
of an EU law it may, and sometimes must, ask the Court of Justice for
advice in a preliminary ruling procedure. Practically, this procedure
works the other way round: you claim in the national court that a
certain national provision contradicts binding EU law – probably the
very EU law which you just tried to lobby in the legislative process

unsuccessfully. Through this mean you can make the Court of Justice check on that very EU law and its legality through the backdoor. The preliminary ruling procedure makes up for more than 50% of the cases of the Court of Justice.

4.2 Actions for failure to fulfil an obligation

The Commission can start these proceedings if it has reason to believe that a Member State is failing to fulfill its obligations under EU law (Art. 226 EC). These proceedings may also be started by another Member State. In either case, the Court of Justice investigates the allegations and gives its judgment. This procedure makes up for about 25% of the court cases. If the Court of Justice finds that the Member State has not complied with its judgment, it may impose a fine on that country in a second step.

4.3 Actions for annulment

If any of the Member States, the Council, the Commission or (under certain conditions) the Parliament believes that a particular EU law is illegal, they may ask the Court of Justice to annul it (Art. 230 EC). Private individuals and stakeholders who want the court to cancel a particular law because it directly and adversely affects them as individuals can also use these actions for annulment. If the court finds that the law in question was not correctly adopted or is not correctly based on the treaties, it may declare the law null and void. This procedure makes up for about 10% of the court cases.

4.4 Actions for failure to act

The Parliament, the Council and the Commission are required to make certain decisions under certain circumstances. If they fail to do so, the Member States, the other EU institutions and (under certain conditions) individuals or companies can lodge a complaint with the Court of Justice so as to have this failure to act officially recorded (Art. 232 EC). However, this procedure makes up for only very few of the court cases.

The remaining 15% of cases the Court of Justice is dealing with are cases of appeal against decisions of the Court of First Instance.

5. The Member States' governments and parliaments

ORGANISATIONAL MAP OF THE GERMAN CHANCELLERY

Chancellor's Office

011	012	013
Speeches and texts	Petitions; Special tasks	Media relations

Angela Merkel

German Chancellor

Staff
Political planning;
Strategic issues;
Special tasks

Office of the Head of the Chancellor's Office

021	022	023
Media Relations Head of the Chancellery	Dialogue with Science	Lagezentrum

Federal Minister
Thomas de Maizière

Head of the Chancellery
Institutional Relations and
Communication Strategy

Department 1	Department 2	Department 3
Central Department; Interior and Justice policy	Foreign-; Security- and Development policy	Social-; Health-; Employment-; Infrastructure and Civil Society policy

Group 11
Personnel administration of the German Federal Government; Administration
Unit 111
Personnel administration of the Chancellery
Unit 112
Budget; Organisation and Controlling
Unit 113
Internal service; Security und protection of classified information
Unit 114 ICT; Copyservice
Unit 115 IFG-Coordination; Visitor's service; Qualification

Group 12
Cabinet, Parliament as well as Bund-Laender affairs Vorhabenerfassung
Unit 121 Cabinet and Parliament
Unit 122 Bund-Laender relations; Bundesrat
Unit 123 Vorhabenerfassung; -planning
Unit 124 Special tasks;
Analysis of opinion research
Unit 125 Research and Documentation
Unit 126 Sports

Group 13
Interior and Justice
Unit 131 Federal Ministry of Justice
Unit132 Federal Ministry of the Interior (except sports)

Group 14
Head of the Bonn Office; Issues regarding the capital

Group 21
Foreign Policy and Global Issues
Unit 211
Security- and Disarmament Policy;
Bilateral relations with the USA, Canada, Northern-, Western-, and Southern Europe and Turkey
Unit 212
Bilateral relations with the states of Central-, East- and Southeast Europe as well as Central Asia and the Transcaucasus
Unit 213
Bilateral relations with the states of the Middle East, Africa, Asia and Latin America
Unit 214
Global Issues; United Nations;
Human rights; Foreign policy issues regarding anti-terrorist measures; Humanitarian help and Cultural policy abroad
Unit 215
Development Policy; North-South Issues
Unit 216
Foreign policy aspects of international economical issues (e.g G8 process or energy); Common Foreign and security policy; European security and defense policy, special tasks

Group 22
Federal Ministery of Defense; German National Security Council
Unit 221
Administration of the Armed Forces; Armament
Unit 222
Military aspects of security policy; German National Security Council

Group 31
Social-, Health-, Employment policy
Unit 311
Social Security, Pension
Unit 312
Health policy
Unit 313
Employment policy; Labour law
Alliance for Employment

Group 32
Infrastructure policy
Unit 321
Federal Ministry for Environment, Nature Conversation and Nuclear Safety; Sustainable development
Unit 322
Federal Ministry of Food, Agriculture and Consumer Protection
Unit 323
Federal Ministry of Transport, Building and Urban Affairs

Group 33
Civil Society policy
Unit 331
Federal Ministry of Education and Research
Unit 332
Federal Ministry for Family, Senior Citizens, Women and Youth; Relations with charities
Unit 333
Relations with Church and religious communities; Special tasks

**Minister of State
Bernd Neumann**

**Federal Commissioner
for Culture and the Media**

Hildegard Müller

Minister of State

**Minister of State
Maria Böhmer**

**Federal Commisioner
for Migration, Refugees and
Integration**

Example for national
government:
German chancellery
and ministries[43]

Department 4 Economic and Financial policy	Department 5 European policy	Department 6 Bundesnachrichtendienst (BND); Federal intelligence service
Group 41 **General Economic Policy** Unit 411 Stratigic economic issues, Economic development; Special tasks Unit 412 SMEs; Trades; Competition; Economic law	**Group 51** **Strategic issues, Relations to** **the EU member states regarding** **European policy** Unit 511 EU-strategic policy issues; EU-Presidency Unit 512 **Relations to the EU member states** **regarding European policy**	**Group 61** **BND strategic issues and legal** **questions; Commissioner for the** **Budget; Parliamentary control of** **intelligence services; Principles of** **Coordination** Unit 611 BND supervision; Personnel; Organisation; Move to Belrin; Legislature relevant to the intelligence services; Security Unit 612 Parliamentary control bodies, Contacts to
Group 42 **Industry; Innovation; Energy;** **Foreign trade; Financial markets** Unit 421 Industry, Telecommunications- and Post; Innovation and Technology; Information Society; Regional economic policy Unit 422 Energy policy, National und international financial markets Unit 423 Foreign trade; G7/G8; Bilateral trade relations	**Group 52** **Coordination of European policy** **including; Economic aspects of the** **European integration** Unit 521 Coordination of the European policy of the German Federal Government; EU financial policy; Economic and monetary union Unit 522 EU economic policy; Internal market; EU structural policy; European law	the Parliament; Principles of Coordina- tion; Relations to the Bundeswehr; G10 Affairs; BND collection and utilisation of informations regarding proliferation and international arms trade
Group 43 **Financial policy; Neue Laender** Unit 431 Budgetary and Financial policy, Federal financial relations Unit 432 Fiscal Policy Unit 433 Coordination of affairs of the Neue Laender		**Group 62** **International situation, Terrorism** **and Organised crime; Assignment** **control; Foreign relations** Unit 621 BND information about regional situa- tions, Assignment control and analysis of information; Foreign relations Unit 622 Intelligence about situations, assignment control and information analysis regard- ing terrorism, extremism and interna- tional organised crime

5.1 Member States in the Council

For you as a lobbyist, the Member States' governments also fulfil an important function with regard to the Council. As mentioned, one minister attends its meetings from each of the EU's national governments. By lobbying national governments, you lobby the Council. This is why you should also focus your efforts on the national Member States capitals and their governments. Lobbying the respective ministers and their staff in their home countries often is a lot easier than addressing them in Brussels. As an EU lobbyist you should therefore always try to have someone lobbying for your stakeholder on the ground in the Member States, too – not only in the EU capital.

Example for national parliament: Plenum of the German Bundestag[44]

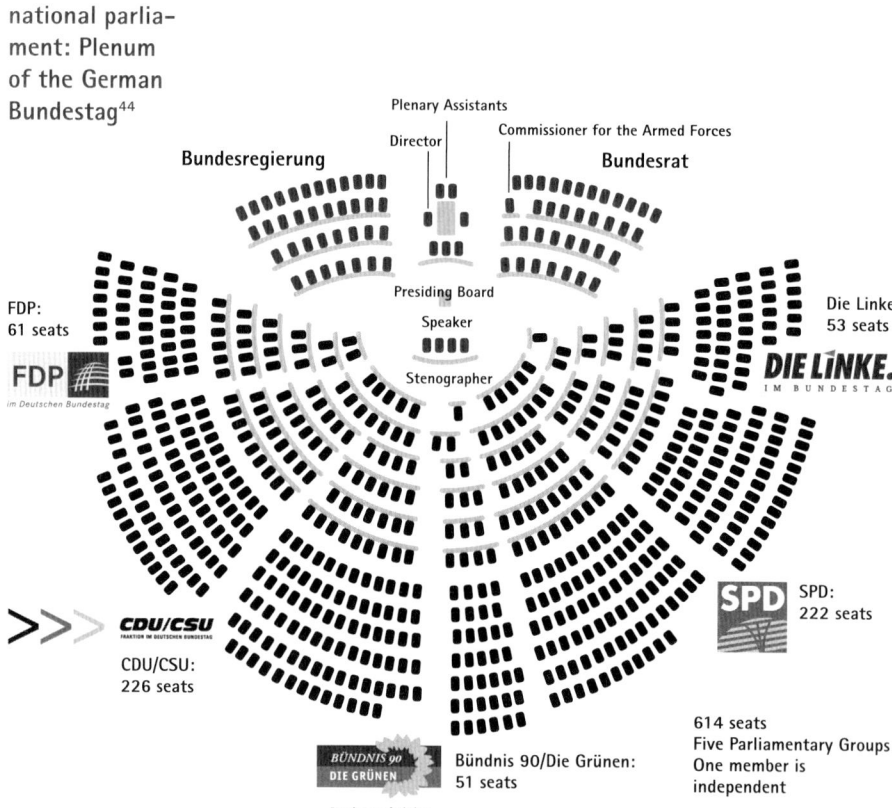

5.2 Member States transforming EU law

Furthermore, regarding the implementation of EU directives into national Member States' laws the governments and parliaments in the
Member States capitals are the only ones to lobby at all. They are
exclusively responsible regarding this transposition of EU legislation:
Directives are frame laws only, which still need transformation into
national Member States' laws. This transformation content usually
is not regulated by the directive very strictly, but provides for a certain bandwidth. In between those parameters, the national legislator
is free to decide on how to implement the directive, setting either
stricter or looser benchmarks. Depending at which end of the scale
your stakeholder's interests are located, you can either lobby for a
very strict or rather loose implementation of the EU benchmarks. This
will be discussed in detail later on.

Tip

When lobbying the
EU, focus on the most
important players:

• European Commission
• European Parliament
• Council of the
  European Union
• European
  Court of Justice
• EU Member
  States Governments

ADDRESSES OF THE FEDERAL MINISTRIES

BERLIN	BONN
Federal Ministry of Labour and Social Affairs Wilhelmstraße 49 10117 Berlin Phone: +49 1888 527-0 Fax: +49 1888 527-4900	**Federal Ministry of Labour and Social Affairs** Rochusstrasse 1 53123 Bonn Phone: +49 1888 527-0 Fax: +49 1888 527-4900
Federal Ministry of Foreign Affairs Werderscher Markt 1 10117 Berlin Postanschrift: 11013 Berlin Phone: +49 30 5000-2858 Fax: +49 30 5000-3866	
Federal Ministry of the Interior Dienstsitz Berlin Alt-Moabit 101 D 10559 Berlin Phone: +49 1888 681-0 Fax: +49 1888 681-2926	**Federal Ministry of the Interior** Graurheindorfer Str. 198 53117 Bonn Phone: +49 1888 681-0 Fax: +49 1888 681-2926
Federal Ministry of Justice Mohrenstraße 37 10117 Berlin Phone: +49 1888 580-9030 Fax: +49 1888 580-9046	**Federal Ministry of Justice** Adenauer Alle 99-103 53113 Bonn Phone: +49 1888 580-0 Fax: +49 1888 580-8325
Federal Ministry of Finance Wilhelmstraße 97 10117 Berlin Phone: +49 1888 682-0 Fax: +49 1888 682-4248	**Federal Ministry of Finance** Graurheindorfer Straße 108 53117 Bonn Phone: +49 1888 682-0 Fax: +49 1888 682-4420
Federal Ministry of Economics and Technology Scharnhorststr. 34-37 10115 Berlin Phone: +49 30 2014-0 Fax: +49 30 2014-5208	**Federal Ministry of Economics and Technology** Villemombler Str. 76 53123 Bonn Phone: +49 228 615-0 Fax: +49 228 615-4436
Federal Ministry of Food, Agriculture and Consumer Protection Wilhelmstr. 54 10117 Berlin Phone: +49 30 2006-0 Fax: +49 30 2006-4262	**Federal Ministry of Food, Agriculture and Consumer Protection** Rochusstr. 1 50123 Bonn Phone: +49 228 529-0 Fax: +49 228 529-4262

ADDRESSES OF THE FEDERAL MINISTRIES

BERLIN	BONN
Federal Ministry of Defence Stauffenbergstraße 18 10785 Berlin Phone: +49 30 2004-0 Fax: +49 30 2004-8333	**Federal Ministry of Defence** Hardthöhe 53125 Bonn Phone: +49 228 120-0 Fax: +49 228 120-5357
Federal Ministry of Family Affairs, Senior Citizens, Woman and Youth Alexanderplatz 6 10178 Berlin Phone: +49 1888 555-0 Fax: +49 1888 555-1145	**Federal Ministry of Family Affairs, Senior Citizens, Woman and Youth** Rochusstraße 8-10 53123 Bonn Phone: +49 1888 555-0 Fax: +49 1888 555-2221
Federal Ministry of Health Friedrichstraße 108 10117 Berlin Phone: +49 1888 441-0 Fax: +49 1888 441-4900	**Federal Ministry of Health** Am Propsthof 78 a 53121 Bonn Phone: +49 1888 441-0 Fax: +49 1888 441-4900
Federal Ministry of Transport, Building and Urban Development Invalidenstraße 44 10115 Berlin Phone: +49 30 2008-0 Fax: +49 30 2008-1942	**Federal Ministry of Transport, Building and Urban Development** Robert-Schumann-Platz 1 53175 Bonn Phone: +49 1888 300-0 Fax: +49 1888 300-3428
Federal Ministry for Environment, Nature Conservation and Nuclear Safety Alexanderplatz 6 10178 Berlin Phone: +49 1888 305-0 Fax: +49 1888 305-4375	**Federal Ministry for Environment, Nature Conservation and Nuclear Safety** Robert-Schuman-Platz 3 53175 Bonn Phone: +49 1888 305-0 Fax: +49 1888 305-3225
Federal Ministry of Education and Research Hannoversche Straße 28-30 10115 Berlin Phone: +49 1888 57-0 Fax: +49 1888 57-83601	**Federal Ministry of Education and Research** Heinemannstr. 2 53175 Bonn Phone: +49 1888 57-0 Fax: +49 1888 57-83601
Federal Ministry of Economic Cooperation and Development Europahaus Stresemannstr. 94 10963 Berlin Phone: +49 1888 535-0 Fax: +49 1888 535-2595	**Federal Ministry of Economic Cooperation and Development** Adenauerallee 139 – 141 53113 Bonn Phone: +49 1888 535-0 Fax: +49 1888 535-3500

IV. How to lobby?

If you want to lobby the EU institutions outlined above effectively and efficiently, you first need to know the legal framework you are working under as a lobbyist. Second, you need to know the legislative procedures that apply in EU law making so you can use the right techniques and tools to influence the decision makers.

The art of lobbying is to achieve congruence of the diverging interests of politics, business and society

Tip

First thing, you should get an accreditation pass to the Parliament to be able to access the building any time you have to. This makes things a lot easier for you.

1. Legal framework

First, you need to know what the formal requirements are if you want to lobby the EU. What is allowed, what is forbidden? How do you gain access?

1.1 Registration and accreditation

At the moment, the Commission does not yet manage a system of formal accreditation nor does it run a compulsory register of those organisations that have dealings with the Commission. However, the Commission has a voluntary database called CONECCS[45] , used for obtaining information on European civil society organisations and their interplay with the EU. It includes trade unions and employer federations, NGOs, consumer groups, organisations representing social and economic players, charitable organisations and community-based organisations. CONECCS can, to a certain extent, be regarded as a database on European lobby groups, though important business lobbyists are not included in it. It is used as an information source for the Commission departments and the general public. The organisations listed in CONECCS are required to have a minimum presence in three

Lobbyist accreditation form European Parliament

Application for general access to the European Parliament for Lobbyists accredited to the European Parliament (Annex I)
(Only the original application form can be accepted)

General information
(Details of this part of the declaration will be set down in a register, made available to the public in the form laid down by the College of Quaestors)
Details about the interest group you are working for:

Name of the organisation

Home adress:

Street: No:

Town: Postcode:

Country:

Tel: GSM:

E-Mail:

Website:

If appropriate please provide the adress of your organisation at one of the working places of the European Parliament if this is different from the home address

Street   No:

Town: Postcode:

Country:

Tel: GSM:

45 http://ec.europa.eu/civil_society/coneccs/index_en.htm

Nature of Organisation' s business (Policy area)
_____

Is the interest group already listed in the register of the European Parliament?
Yes   No
(If not, please attach document for registration)
                    □
Is the interest group listed in the register of the European Commission?
Yes   No
_____
General information about you
Surname:
Given names:
Nationality: □   □   □
Language to be used for further correspondence
    EN   FR   DE   NL
Home address: □
Street: No:
Town: Postcode:
Country:
Tel: GSM:
E-Mail:
(Please attach a copy of ID card or passport showing place of residance and a copy of a Certificate
of good conduct of the country of residence)

Personal position's function in the interest group   □
□   □

Please attach a document showing your relationship with the interest group. If the relationship is a
temporary relationship please clarify the period

Period of access requested (maximum one year)
3 months   6 months   9 months   1 year

Have you ever hab long-term access to the European Parliament before?
Yes   No

Expiry date of the previous access card
_____

Additional information
(will not be made public; only to be used for the European Parliament's internal administrative purposes)

Purpose of requesting general access to the European Parliament

Visiting European Parliament premises in:

BRU □   Regularly □   sometimes □   no

STR □   Regularly □   sometimes □   no

LUX □   Regularly □   sometimes □   no

Following European Parliament sessions in:

BRU □   Regularly □   sometimes □   no

STR □   Regularly □   sometimes □   no

Following meetings of parliamentary committies

Regularly □   sometimes □   no □

Parliamentary committees most frequently attended:

1.
2.
3.

Using other facilities of the European Parliament
Visiting library of the European Parliament

Regularly □   sometimes □   no □

Using other infrastructure available in th European Paliament

Regularly □   sometimes □   no □

If yes, please clarify which

Member States and to provide information on the following: financing, countries in which they operate, objectives, policy areas and chief staff, which is then displayed on the Internet.

The registration process is done online, i.e. the organisations themselves feed the data into the system. They also have to update the information on a regular basis and risk being removed from the database if they fail to do so. At the moment, CONECCS contains information about almost 740 European organisations[46]. While CONECCS aids efforts at transparency, there is no requirement or substantial incentive for a civil society organisation to be registered. Equally there is no great disincentive for failing to do so. A lack of an enforcement mechanism means that the information provided is frequently outdated. The Commission already tried to put some pressure on the lobby groups in the past to encourage the use of CONECCS, in order to increase transparency, by stating that lobbyists submitting comments on a policy proposal must provide the Commission with the information on who they are and who they represent, since otherwise submissions will be considered as individual contributions only. But this did not lead to much success[47]. However, the latest transparency initiative of the Commission is expected to change that and lead to a compulsory system of registration and accreditation.

The Parliament already has such a system of accreditation[48] for lobbyists. Access passes ("badges") for lobbyists are issued by the security department of the Parliament[49] and are valid for one year. To apply for such a pass you need to fill in the following form stating your name, the name of the firm you work for, the reason why you need access, along

[46] Commission staff working document, Report of the inter-departmental working group on a possible "European Transparency Initiative", (SEC(2005) 1300 final), p. 12
[47] Communication on general principles and minimum standards for consultation of interested parties, COM (2002) 704; [48] "Rule of Procedure of the European Parliament, Annex IX : Provisions governing the application of Rule 9(4) - Lobbying in Parliament; [49] Email: SecuLongTermPass@europarl.eu.int

with several other documents like a copy of the ID etc. After the application has been approved by the so-called Quaestors, who are MEPs charged with this administrative task, you have to pick up your pass in the Parliament where a photograph of you is taken and both inserted into the database of the Parliament and into your access pass. According to the Parliament, lobbyists can be private, public or non-governmental bodies to provide the Parliament with knowledge and specific expertise in numerous economic, social, environmental and scientific areas.

The Parliament's register of accredited lobbyists is published on the Parliament website[50]. It is simply an alphabetical list and only provides the name of the badge holders and the organisation they represent. It does not give any indication of the interests for which a lobbyist is acting.

Sticking to those formal requirements of accreditation will open doors a lot easier for you as far as administrative burdens are concerned.

Information about the nature of the work

Direct involvement in legislative preparatory work
Yes   No
If yes, please explain:

Relations within the European Parliament:
MEPs:
If yes, are there MEPs you can name as reference:
1.
2.
3.
Committee and delegation secretariats:
If yes, please indicate which ones:
1.
2.
3.
Others:
If yes, please clarify:

Relations outside the European Parliament, linked to the work as lobbyist:
National parliament/government:
NGOs:
Trade associations' companies:
Others (please clarify):

Request for a permanent access card (possible in case of more than 50 visits a year)
Yes   No
This declaration is made under personal responsibility of the applicant and must be renewed every year.

The follow up of your application for a visitor's access requires the recording of your personal data (data, time, place of entries) in a file.
Should you require further information or exercise your rights (e.g. to access or rectify data), please contact the Accreditation center of the Security Unit, ASP OLEXXXX, European Parliament, rue Wirtz, B-1047 Brussels.

I undertake to adhere to the code of the conduct drawnup by the European Parliament and to other relevant provisions.

Signature:
Place and Date:

Space reserved for use by the Administration	

1.2 Code of Conduct

It is essential for you to keep in mind the overall legal framework under which the representatives of the European institutions and the lobbyists are operating.

There are two sets of hard law, which are relevant in this context. First and foremost, in case of serious misbehaviour like bribery and corruption both groups can be subject to sanctions under the penal codes of the countries in which the European institutions have their seat. Secondly, staff members of all European institutions and bodies are subject to additional rules according to the staff regulation, which has the objective to ensure the integrity of the European public service. Failure to respect these rules can result in disciplinary procedures. So, the traditional concept has been putting the focus on the ethical behaviour of the EU institutions rather than establishing a conduct for lobbyists, since bribery has not been an issue in the EU institutions so far. Up until now, the Commission has therefore opted for a self-regulation policy[51] and invited lobbyists to adopt their own codes of conduct on the basis of minimal criteria proposed by the Commission[52].

Commission Code of Conduct 1

EU lobbyists shall
- identify themselves by name and by company
- declare the interest represented
- neither intentionally misrepresent their status nor the nature of their inquiries to officials of the EU institutions nor create any false impression in relation thereto
- neither directly nor indirectly misrepresent links with EU institutions
- honour confidential information given to them
- not disseminate false or misleading information knowingly or recklessly and shall exercise proper care to avoid doing so inadvertently
- not sell for profit to third parties copies of documents obtained from EU institutions
- not obtain information from EU institutions by dishonest means
- avoid any professional conflicts of interest
- neither directly nor indirectly offer nor give any financial inducement to any EU official, nor Member of the Parliament, nor their staff

---

[51] Communication on an open and structured dialogue between the Commission and special interest groups, OJ C 63 of 5/3/1993
[52] http://ec.europa.eu/commission_barroso/kallas/doc/transp_report_en.pdf

- neither propose nor undertake any action which would constitute an improper influence on them
- only employ EU personnel subject to the rules and confidentiality requirements of the EU institution

Commission Code of Conduct 2

- Commissioners may not engage in any other professional activity, whether paid or unpaid. Commissioners may hold honorary, unpaid posts in non-profit-making organisations or associations. These posts shall under no circumstances involve any risk of a conflict of interest and shall be listed in a declaration. The declaration must relate to activities engaged in over the last ten years and must distinguish between activities that ended before the Commissioner took up office and those that will continue after that point.
- Commissioners must declare any financial interest or asset, which might create a conflict of interests in the performance of their duties. The declaration shall include any holdings by the Commissioner's spouse, which might entail a conflict of interests.
- Commissioners shall not accept any gift with a value of more than € 150.-. When, in accordance with diplomatic usage, they receive gifts worth more than this amount, they shall hand them over to the Commission's Protocol department. The Commission's Protocol department keeps a public register of gifts with a value of more than € 150.-.
- When Commissioners intend to engage in an occupation during the year after they have ceased to hold office, they must inform the Commission in good time. The Commission will then examine the nature of the planned occupation. The Commission seeks the opinion of an ad hoc ethical committee. In the light of the committee findings, the Commission will decide.

In the course of the Abramoff scandal in Washington and the massive impact on the lobbying scene in the US, the rules will probably also be tightened and more specific on EU level, as indicated by the Commission through its latest transparency initiative[53].

The Parliament, however, has a compulsory code of conduct for all those wishing to seek accreditation[54]. This code of conduct is similar in nature to the model proposed by the Commission. Any breach may lead to the withdrawal of parliamentary access and accreditation.

[53] Green Paper on European Transparency Initiative: http://ec.europa.eu/commission_barroso/kallas/doc/com2006_0194_4_en.pdf
[54] Contained in Article 3 of Annex IX to the EP's Rules of Procedure

The ethical behaviour of Members of the Parliament is governed by the provisions of the Rules of Procedure[55], which the Parliament has given itself.

Parliament Code of Conduct

- Every MEP with a direct financial interest in the area under debate has to declare this orally.
- The Quaestors hold a register of all declarations of MEPs on their remunerated activities and the support they receive from third parties. The register is open to the public for inspection. The President of the Parliament can suspend an MEP if he refuses to submit a declaration of interests.
- MEPs shall refrain from accepting any other gift or benefit in the performance of their duties.

If, as a lobbyist, you stick to those few rules of formal behaviour, you will avoid ruining your reputation and the one of your counterparts.

2. Legislative procedures

In most cases, you as a lobbyist will turn to the EU institutions regarding a new draft law or policy on the horizon. There is no use in doing so if you do not know how the policy becomes a law, i.e. how the legislative process in the EU works.

Example

In May 2000 the Commission proposed two new directives[56] to revise the rules governing public procurement in the EU. The drafts were the follow up of a Green Paper on the subject published in 1996 and a Communication on policy priorities in 1998.

Lobbyist X was involved in that process almost from the beginning. Being concerned about certain aspects of the proposed law changes regarding his stakeholder, X responded to both the Green Paper and the following Communication with detailed fact information giving reason and argument why certain ideas of the Commission were not ideal and what he

[55] Annexes I and IX; [56] Proposal for a directive on the coordination of procedures for the award of public supply contracts, public service contracts and public works contracts, COM(2000)275; Proposal for a directive on the coordination of the procurement procedures of entities operating in the water, energy and transport sectors, COM(2000)276

suggested instead. X talked to the case handler in the Commission based on his written arguments he had handed in before. He had no alternative political access to the Commission (no personal connection to the Head of Unit or political link to the respective Commissioner in charge) so he had to focus exclusively on the working level.

Since the statements X made did not fall on fruitful ground in the Commission, X focused his lobbying efforts on the Parliament[57]. X first made a position paper on the subject. The responsible committee within the Parliament was the Legal Affairs and Internal Market Committee. The Environment Committee, Social Affairs Committee and Economic and Monetary Committee were responsible for preparing opinions on the proposal. X had a first meeting with the rapporteur from the Legal Affairs Committee, Mr Zappalà (PPE) in December 2000. X also took part in a Parliament hearing in January 2001. On that basis X made a "proposal list" of amendments to the directives in February 2001 containing amendments which he regarded as necessary for his purposes. X then sent the amendment proposals to the rapporteur as well as to the shadow rapporteurs for each group and the co-ordinators responsible for the Legal Affairs Committee within each group. X also sent the amendments to the rapporteurs responsible for the opinions in the other committees as well as to other MEPs engaged in this issue.

Between April and June 2001, X arranged a first set of meetings with the shadow rapporteurs and coordinators in the Legal Affairs Committee, for the principal political groups (other than PPE): PSE (Berger (A), Medina Ortega (Sp)), ELDR (Wallis (UK), Thors (S)), Greens (Hautala (SF)). Most MEPs showed a keen interest in X's amendments and suggested to table some of them for the vote of the report in committee. The amendments tabled in the Legal Affairs Committee by the opinion rapporteurs and individual MEPs later contained most of X's amendments. On this basis, X drew up a voting list. The voting list was sent by e-mail and fax to all members of the Legal Affairs Committee a few days before the vote. Many of X's amendments were adopted in committee. However, a number of inconsistent amendments were adopted on some of the important issues. X therefore prepared some proposals for compromise amendments on that basis, which were sent to all the relevant MEPs. X then organised a second set of meetings with MEPs in December 2001, before the plenary vote, to ensure that the amendments voted in committee would be carried through in plenary, and that those that didn't get through would be tabled again. The Parliament, which had co-decision powers on this issue, finally adopted several of those amendments to the proposal in January 2002.

The Commission therefore presented a modified version of the proposal in May 2002. X then sent his position papers and amendments to the

Permanent Representations in Brussels and made contact with the person responsible for this issue within the Danish Permanent Representation. X also sent the amendments to the governments in the Member States. The Council reached a respective agreement on the directives in May 2002.

When is the right time for which arguments? That depends on which EU institution you lobby. And when is the right time to talk to whom in which institution? That depends on the applicable legislative procedure, which again depends on the legislative subject in question[58]. To know which player to target in which of the EU institutions at what time in the legislative process to achieve the desired goal is the key to lobbying success. It is therefore crucial for a lobbyist to understand the different ways of EU law making in detail.

The different acts of EU law are covered by Art. 249 EC. They consist of so-called regulations, directives, decisions, recommendations and opinions.

◀

Tip

To be able to lobby effectively and not be limited to small talk and champagne, you need to know the different forms of EU law and the exact legislative procedures that apply for them. Only then can you intervene efficiently in the EU legislative process.

A regulation is in fact comparable to a law, i.e. a general measure that is binding in all its parts. Unlike directives, which are addressed to the Member States, and decisions, which are for specified recipients, regulations are addressed to everyone. A regulation is directly applicable, which means that it creates law which takes immediate effect in all the Member States in the same way as a national law, without any further action on the part of the national authorities.

A directive, however, is a frame law addressed to the Member States. Its main purpose is to align national legislation. A directive is binding on the Member States as to the result to be achieved but leaves them the choice of the form and method they adopt to realise the objectives within the framework of their internal legal order. If a directive has not been transposed into national legislation in a Member State, if it has been transposed incompletely or if there is a delay in transposing it, citizens can directly invoke the directive in question before the national courts.

A decision is the instrument by which the EU institutions give a ruling on a particular matter. By means of a decision, the institutions can require a Member State or a citizen of the EU to take or refrain from taking a particular action, or confer rights or impose obligations on a Member State or a citizen. A decision is an individual measure, and the persons to whom it is addressed must be specified individually, which distinguishes a decision from a regulation.

[58] http://europa.eu.int/eur-lex/en/about/abc/abc_21.html

A recommendation on the other hand allows the EU institutions to make their views known and to suggest a line of action without imposing any legal obligation on those to whom it is addressed (the Member States, other institutions, or in certain cases the citizens of the EU).

An opinion is an instrument that allows the EU institutions to make a statement in a non-binding fashion, in other words without imposing any legal obligation on those to whom it is addressed. The aim is to set out an EU institution's point of view on an issue[59].

For your legislative lobbying efforts, the regulations and directives are especially important. As far as administrative lobbying is concerned, especially regarding competition law issues, the decisions of the Commission are of importance. The respective EU law making procedures to implement those measures are laid down in the relevant policy chapters and most importantly in Art. 251 and 252 EC. The lack of procedural knowledge of the EC Treaty is quite common among lobbyists which is why most lobbyists are making the same mistakes in their lobbying: Providing inappropriate briefing materials, being too early or too late with their lobbying, failing to understand EU processes and procedures or approaching the wrong person. A new survey among the EU decision makers supports this[60], though opinions diverge in detail.

While the Parliament and the Commission rate NGO lobbying marginally more effective than industry's, Council officials believe industry is slightly more effective. Overall, though, Commission, Parliament and Council rate both industry and NGOs as equally (in-)effective. Member State governments and EU institutions themselves, however, have a crucial impact on decision makers in other EU institutions.

EU laws to lobby are regulations and directives

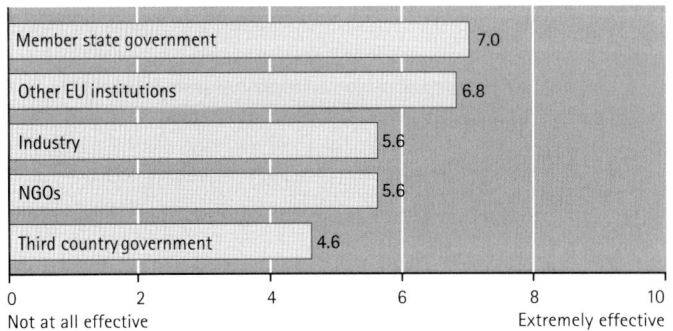

Effectiveness of Lobbying

(?) How would you rate the effectiveness of lobbying of the following organisations?

[59] http://eur-lex.europa.eu/en/droit_communautaire/droit_communautaire.htm
[60] Burson-Marsteller, The Definitive Guide to Lobbying the European Institutions, p. 5

They lobby more effectively than industry and NGOs. Third country governments achieve the lowest effectiveness of lobbying. While industry is also criticised for basing its arguments on positions that are too national, the highest score for an example of bad lobbying tactics goes to NGOs' tendency to base their positions on emotion rather than facts. The finding that NGOs too often base a position on emotion is by no means a blanket criticism. The data shows that MEPs, no doubt because they are political campaigners with an instinctive sympathy for the value of clear messages, have a greater preference for the NGOs' approach. Both industry and NGO lobbyists are often criticised the most for being too aggressive or being insufficiently transparent. Offering unethical inducements, however, is the least common example of poor lobbying among industry and NGOs[61].

If you want to do a better job for your stakeholder, get familiar with the EU's legislative procedures. Here they are:

2.1 Consultation procedure

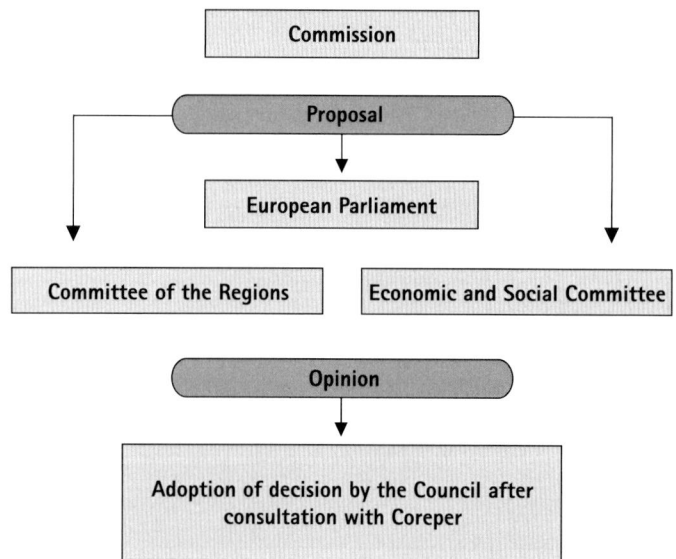

You need to know that powers in the consultation procedure are shared between the Commission and the Council: the Commission submits proposals and the Council makes the decisions. However, the Parliament, and in some cases the Economic and Social Committee and the Committee of the Regions, have to be consulted.

The consultation procedure applies, for example, regarding laws on discrimination, the agricultural policy (which makes up for almost 50% of the EU budget), liberalisation of certain services, competition and taxation, employment policies, extension of foreign trade policy, social security, protection of workers' interests and the improvement of working conditions, provisions in the environmental field relating to fiscal matters, town and country planning, land use or water management, as well as measures concerning a Member State's choice between different energy sources and the general structure of its energy supply[62].

Powers are shared between Commission and Council

While the Parliament can ask for legislative action, the Commission sets the machinery in motion. A legislative proposal is prepared, under a Commissioner's responsibility, by the department dealing with the particular policy field. The department consults national experts at this stage. This sometimes takes the form of deliberations in specially convened committees. Alternatively, experts may have questions put to them by the relevant departments of the Commission. In practice, this consultation is particularly important in that it enables the Commission, while it is still in the process of drawing up a proposal, to assess its chances of being approved by the Council and, if necessary, seek compromises at this early stage. The draft drawn up by the Commission, setting out the content and form of the measure to the last detail, goes before the Commission as a whole when a simple majority is enough to have it adopted. It is now a "Commission proposal", and is sent to the Council with detailed explanatory remarks.

By way of consultation, the Council officially forwards the Commission's proposal to the President of the Parliament and formally requests Parliament to set out its position. The President passes the proposal on to the relevant committee of Parliament for further consideration. The outcome of the committee's deliberations is then discussed at a plenary session of the Parliament, and is set out in a report, which may accept or reject the proposal or propose amendments. The Council is not legally obliged to take account of the opinions or amendments emanating from the Parliament. After the Parliament, the Economic and Social Committee and the Committee of the Regions have been

[62] http://europa.eu.int/eur-lex/en/about/abc/abc_21.html

consulted, the Commission proposal is once more put before the Council - perhaps amended by the Commission in the light of the opinions of Parliament and the committees – where it is discussed by the Permanent Representatives Committee (Coreper). In the Coreper, specialised working groups work out all the technical details of decisions to be taken by the Council in advance. As described in detail above, as soon as a measure is ready for adoption, it is entered as an "A item" on the agenda of the next Council meeting and is adopted without further debate. If, however, there are irreconcilable differences of opinion within the Coreper about the actual provisions of the measure concerned, the outstanding issues are entered on the agenda as "B items" for further discussion by the Council in order to find a solution. Adoption of the proposal by the Council is the final stage in the legislative process.

2.2 Approval procedure

Prior approval
of Parliament

The principal form of Parliament's involvement in the legislative process is the approval procedure, whereby a legal instrument can only be adopted with the prior approval of Parliament. This procedure does not, however, give Parliament any scope for directly influencing the nature of the legal provisions. For example, it cannot propose any amendments or secure their acceptance during the approval procedure. Its role is restricted to accepting or rejecting the legal instrument submitted to it.

Provision is made for this procedure in connection with the accession of new Member States, the conclusion of association agreements and other cornerstone agreements with non-member countries, the transfer of further specific tasks to the European Central Bank (ECB), amendments to the Statute of European System of Central Banks (ESCB) and the appointment of the President of the Commission and the members of the Commission as a body.

2.3 Cooperation procedure

In practice, this procedure is only relevant in relation to the economic and monetary union. In all other scenarios in which it was used, it has now been replaced by the co-decision procedure. The cooperation procedure basically introduces a Second Reading by the Parliament and the Council into the legislative process.

First Reading

The procedure begins with a Commission proposal, which is sent not only to the Council, but also to the Parliament. The idea behind Parliament's involvement at this early stage is to give it an opportunity, in the interests of effective participation in the legislative process, to give the Council its views on the Commission proposal before the common position is drawn up. The Economic and Social Committee and the Committee of the Regions may also be consulted at this stage.

On the basis of the opinions submitted, the Council then adopts, by qualified majority, a common position. This sets out the Council's position in the light of the Commission's proposal and the opinions. It is therefore not a compromise document but rather a reflection of the Council's view arrived at independently.

Second Reading

The common position is then sent to the Parliament for its Second Reading. The Parliament has three months to take one of the following courses of action.

- If the Parliament accepts the common position or gives no response within the deadline, the Council adopts the common position.
- The Parliament may, however, reject the common position or propose amendments. In either case, the Council may proceed with its adoption, albeit in two different ways. If the common position is rejected, unanimity is required for adoption by the Council. Given the difficulty of achieving unanimity in the Council, the proposal is effectively blocked. Only rarely will the Parliament block legislation in this way. The Parliament usually proposes amendments. The question is then whether the Commission accepts the amendments. If it does, the Council may adopt the instrument in the usual way, by a qualified majority or (if it is departing from the Commission's proposal) unanimously. If the Commission does not accept the Parliament's amendments, their adoption by the Council requires a unanimous vote. The Parliament has to get the Commission on its side in order to lend weight to its arguments. In any event, the Council may still exercise a veto by not taking any decision on the amendments proposed by the Parliament or on the amended Commission proposal, thereby blocking the legislation in question.

2.4 Co-decision procedure

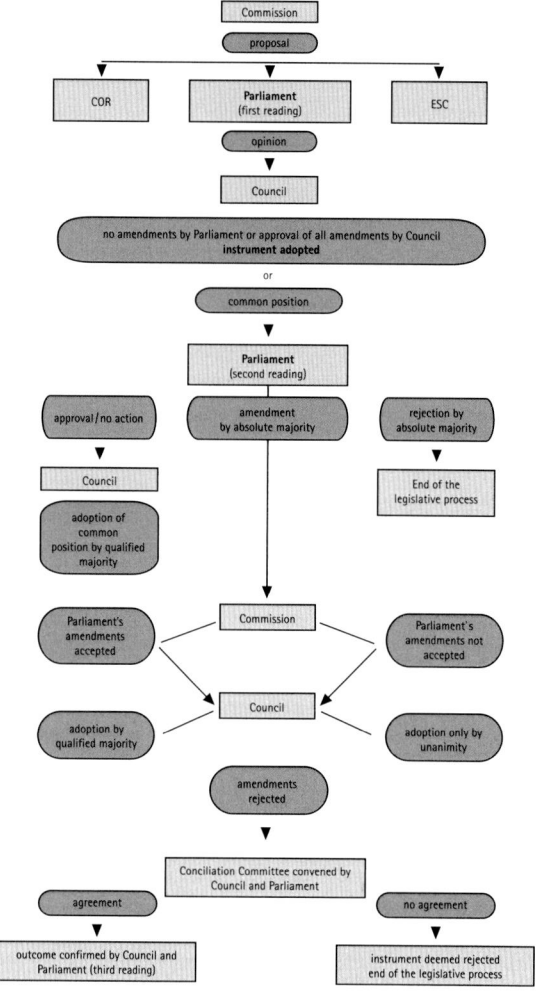

This is the procedure, which you will probably deal most with. It applies to the majority of policy issues most lobbyists have to deal with. Whilst the Council may unanimously override Parliament's views under the cooperation procedure, the co-decision procedure creates "equality of arms" between Council and Parliament. The co-decision procedure denies the Council the right to adopt its common position if efforts to reach agreement with the Parliament fail. This increases the incentive to reach a compromise, as the entire legislative process must otherwise be abandoned.

The co-decision procedure has become by far the most important element in the legislative process. It is used, for example, regarding discrimination on grounds of nationality, the exercise of the right of residence, measures to bring about freedom of movement, directives on freedom of establishment, freedom to provide services, transport policy, creation of the single market, social policy, public health, consumer protection, trans-European networks, regional funds, research and environmental protection programmes. It works as follows[63]:

First Reading
Starting point is a Commission proposal that is sent to the Council, the Parliament and any committees to be consulted. The Parliament takes its First Reading and sends its opinion to the Council. The Economic and Social Committee and the Committee of the Regions are also given an opportunity to set out their position at this stage. If the Parliament does not make any amendments to the Commission's proposal, or the Commission accepts all amendments proposed by the Parliament, the instrument may be adopted at this stage of the procedure. Otherwise, a Second Reading before the Parliament is required.

Second Reading
On the basis of the Commission's proposal and Parliament's and the committees' opinions and its own deliberations, the Council adopts a common position by a qualified majority. The common position is then sent to the Parliament for its Second Reading. Parliament now has three months in which to do one of three things.
- If the Parliament accepts the Council's common position or gives no response within three months, the law is deemed to have been adopted as set out in the common position.
- If the Parliament makes amendments to the Council's common position, the Council has the opportunity to adopt the common position as amended by the Parliament, in which case all the proposed changes must be accepted. If, however, the Council rejects certain amendments or the majority needed for their adoption cannot be obtained, then the President of the Council must, within six weeks, convene a so-called Conciliation Committee (see Third Reading) to consider the Council's common position in the light of the Parliament's proposed amendments[64]. The aim is to achieve a workable compromise which can be adopted by the required majorities in the Council and the Parliament.

[63] http://europa.eu.int/eur-lex/en/about/abc/abc_21.html
[64] http://www.europarl.europa.eu/code/information/what_is_en.htm

- If the Parliament rejects the common position outright (for which an absolute majority of MEPs is required), the legislative process is at an end.

Main differences between the first and the second reading[65]

First reading	no time limits; proposal considered by committee responsible and opinion giving committees; broad admissibility criteria for amendments; Parliament adopts amendments by a simple majority
Second reading	strict time limits of 3–4 months; common position considered only by the committee responsible; strict admissibility criteria for amendments; Parliament adopts amendments with the absolute majority of its members (i. e. at least 367 votes)

Conciliation Committee and Third Reading

The results of the Parliament's Second Reading vote are transmitted to the Council. From the time of receipt, it has three months (or four, if extended) to complete its Second Reading by deciding whether or not it can accept all Parliament's Second Reading amendments. In practice, the Council unofficially informs Parliament as soon as possible whether it can accept them or not. The Council acts throughout the whole co-decision procedure by qualified majority, except in the areas of the EC Treaty articles 42 (freedom of movement for workers), 47(2) (measures concerning the self-employed persons) and 151(5) (incentive measures in respect of culture) where unanimity is required. However, up until the formal conclusion of the Second Reading phase, the Council needs unanimity to accept any Parliament amendments on which the Commission has delivered a negative opinion.

The Conciliation Committee

If the Council objects to any amendment, a so-called Conciliation Committee has to be convened. The Conciliation Committee leads direct negotiations between the two co-legislating institutions (the Parliament and the Council). Conciliation is then normally followed by the final adoption of the draft at the Third Reading[66]. The Conciliation Committee consists of two delegations: the Council delegation, composed of the 25 members of the Council or their representatives, and the Parliament delegation composed of an equal number of MEPs. On the basis of the Parliament's current political party composition[67], the EPP-ED is represented in the Parliament delegation with 10 members,

[65] http://www.europarl.europa.eu/code/information/guide_en.pdf
[66] http://www.europarl.europa.eu/code/information/guide_en.pdf
[67] See chapter „Who is lobbied?"

First and second reading agreements:
guidelines for best practice within Parliament

Preliminary considerations

1. Committees should make full use of the possibilities provided by the Treaties that allow for up to three readings. The decision to seek to achieve a first or second reading agreement should take due account of the very different situations existing at the first and second reading stages respectively. This concerns in particular the extent to which Parliament and Council have already reached a formal position; the majorities required at plenary stage and the deadlines imposed by the Treaties.

2. The decision should receive broad political support and should be taken in a transparent manner and announced in committee. It should be justified in terms of political priorities, deadlines, risk of legal uncertainty, or the uncontroversial nature of the proposal.

Meetings with Council and Commission

3. Informal contacts should be possible at all stages, provided that the committee, coordinators or shadow rapporteurs are kept informed of their existence and content. Concrete negotiations should not usually take place until the committee has adopted its first or second reading amendments. This position can then provide the mandate on the basis of which the committee's representatives can negotiate with Council and Commission.

4. EP participation should be decided by the coordinators. It should permit the fullest possible information to be provided to all political groups within the committee, either through direct participation of the Committee Chair and/or shadow rapporteurs or coordinators, or through prompt and sufficiently detailed information from the rapporteur to the Chair and shadow rapporteurs or coordinators. The coordinators may decide to invite the opinion committee draftsman to participate.

5. Interpretation should be provided, if requested, in particular during the concrete negotiation phase after the vote in committee.

6. Draft compromise texts submitted by any institution, and which are to be the basis of discussion at a forthcoming meeting, should as far as possible be circulated in advance to all negotiators.

Follow-up to meetings

7. The rapporteur should report back regularly on the state of negotiations, if necessary to the whole committee. Any significant change in the negotiating position should have broad political support.

8. The Council Presidency should be encouraged to participate in committee meetings to present the Council position.

9. If an agreement is reached, the Council Presidency should be invited to send a letter to the Committee Chair confirming Council's agreement in principle, and annexing the text.

10. Any compromise amendments required as a result of the agreement reached should be the subject of written information to all committee members. If they can not be approved by the committee for submission to plenary, they should be co-signed by the rapporteur and shadow rapporteurs or coordinators on behalf of their political groups to demonstrate that the amendments enjoy broad support.

Parliament guidelines for First and Second Reading

the PES with 8, the ALDE with 3 and the Greens/EFA, the GUE/NGL, the IND/DEM and the UEN with one member each. The Conciliation Committee has to be convened within six weeks (or eight, if extended) after the Council has concluded its Second Reading and has notified the Parliament that it is not in a position to accept all the latter's Second Reading amendments. The Conciliation Committee is constituted separately for each legislative proposal requiring conciliation and has at its disposal six weeks (or eight, if extended), to reach an overall agreement in the form of a joint text. In fulfilling this task, it is required to address the text of the common position on the basis of the Parliament's Second Reading amendments, which together form the basis for the conciliation procedure.

The Commission also takes part in the proceedings with a view to reconciling the positions of the Parliament and the Council. If the Conciliation Committee does not reach an agreement, or if the Parliament or the Council do not approve the joint text in the Third Reading, the draft is deemed not to have been adopted. In this case the co-decision procedure can only be restarted with a new legislative proposal from the Commission.

Conciliation provides you as a lobbyist with an additional possibility to lobby all of the EU institutions. Use it. Each of the procedure steps which are clearly and formally defined gives you an access door at a certain time.

At the constituent meeting, there is often a short exchange of views on the substance of the issues at stake, with the participation of the Commission representatives, particularly when the first reaction of the Council to Parliament's Second Reading amendments is known. The Commission is present at all meetings of the Parliament delegation since it is expected to present and explain the Commission's opinion on Parliament's Second Reading amendments. At the constituent meeting of the delegation, the members will find in their files a so-called basic document concerning the conciliation procedure in question. This contains the initial Commission proposal, the Parliament amendments from the First Reading, the amended Commission proposal, the Council's Common Position, the Parliament amendments from the Second Reading and the opinion of the Commission, if available. For each delegation meeting, the secretariat draws up a note for members, summarising the aims of the meeting, the situation concerning the amendments, the stage of negotiations with the Council and the procedural aspects. The secretariat also draws up a summary record of each delegation meeting.

The "trialogue"   When the Council is ready to present its position on the Parliament amendments, whether it has formally concluded its Second Reading or not, an informal, tripartite meeting between the Parliament, the Council and the Commission, known as a "trialogue", is arranged. The Parliament negotiating team mandated by the delegation represents Parliament, whereas the Deputy Permanent Representative (Chair of Coreper) of the Member State holding the Presidency represents the Council. The Directorate General in question participates in the meeting on the Commission's behalf. The number of people attending is limited to the negotiating team plus the essential support staff (normally no more than 10 persons from each institution) to ensure the effectiveness of these meetings. All members of the Parliament delegation receive, for their advance information, details of each trialogue (timing, participants and venue), even when not invited to attend themselves.

At the first trialogue, the Presidency representative gives the Council's position on the Parliament amendments, accepting perhaps some of them, rejecting some and proposing compromise texts on others. Positions are discussed and explained and further compromise texts can be drafted, subject to subsequent approval in the respective delegations.

The negotiations in the trialogues are conducted on the basis of a joint so-called four-column working document. The first two columns present the original positions of the Council (common position) and of the Parliament (amendments from the Second Reading). In the third column is inserted the Council's reaction to these Parliament amendments. The position of the Parliament's delegation is placed in the fourth column. These last two columns may be modified several times during the conciliation procedure in order to reflect the evolution of the negotiations.

The trialogues can ask that more technical preparations or drafting work be done in a working party at a political level (for instance the Parliament rapporteur meeting the Council working group Chair) or at the level of civil servants. Due to the growing number of meetings required and the strict time limits, these informal meetings in various compositions are becoming more common. The Commission is often invited to produce compromise texts to be discussed in the respective delegations or at the next trialogue meeting. The results of the trialogues are discussed and possibly approved at the meetings of the respective delegations and further trialogues or informal meetings arranged where necessary. After each trialogue, and in advance of the forth-coming delegation meeting, members of the delegation are informed that the trialogue took place, which members attended, and whether there was any major concrete development. They also receive, where appropriate, an updated version of the joint four-column working document and any compromise texts presented at the trialogue.

Trialogue meetings take place regularly throughout the conciliation procedure with the aim of sorting out the outstanding issues and preparing the ground for the reaching of an agreement in the Conciliation Committee. Normally a short trialogue meeting is held just before the meeting of the Conciliation Committee and sometimes the Conciliation Committee meeting itself is interrupted for negotiations in trialogue to clarify the situation, to find mutually acceptable compromises and to avoid misunderstandings between the delegations[68].

After the first trialogue or other informal contacts, the Chair convenes the Parliament delegation to discuss the results of the negotia-

[68] http://www.europarl.europa.eu/code/information/guide_en.pdf

tions. Normally these meetings are held during a plenary session or in conjunction with a parliamentary committee meeting. The deliberations of the Parliament delegations to the Conciliation Committee are open to all those working inside the Parliament, but are not open to the public. The political groups, the relevant services of the Parliament and the Commission are formally invited to attend the meetings. The Council does not attend these meetings. At such meetings the negotiating team informs the other members of the Parliament delegation of the results of the trialogue(s) and the delegation receives the position of the Council in the form of the joint four-column working document. The delegation also considers compromise texts discussed at or drafted after the trialogue(s). The Commission representatives who are present at the meeting can respond to requests for more detailed information. They may also be able to give some details about the meeting of Coreper where the Council has discussed the results of the trialogue. The main aim of the delegation meetings is to adopt a strategy vis-à-vis the Council position at every stage of the procedure as well as to discuss any compromise texts. Agreement concerning certain amendments or compromise proposals is given, if appropriate, subject to overall agreement. If outstanding questions remain, the delegation gives instructions to the negotiating team to pursue negotiations with the Council. Delegation meetings are usually organised shortly after the trialogue meetings or whenever the development of the conciliation procedure so requires. Like trialogues, a delegation meeting always precedes the meeting of the Conciliation Committee and is also organised if the Conciliation Committee meeting is interrupted for negotiations in a trialogue. At the end of the conciliation procedure, the delegation formally approves or rejects the agreement reached. The delegation aims to act by consensus. However, if a vote is needed, an absolute majority of members is required.

"A" items and "B" items   In the official calendar of the Parliament[69], certain dates are reserved for these meetings. These dates are marked with a circle. Other dates can be arranged subject to the agreement of the two institutions. A short trialogue and meetings of the delegations normally precede a full Conciliation Committee meeting. The Vice President of the Parliament chairing the Parliament delegation and the Minister or Secretary of State holding the Presidency-in-Office of the Council, co-chair the Conciliation Committee meetings. The meeting is opened by the co-chair from the host institution. The Commissioner responsible represents the Commission. At a single meeting of the Conciliation Committee, several dossiers can be on the agenda:

- "A" items, either to open the conciliation procedure or formally to mark the agreement on those legislative proposals, where the delegations have reached an overall agreement already during informal negotiations and subsequent meetings of the delegations. There is no discussion in the Conciliation Committee on these items.

- "B" items. They are the principal theme of discussion since full agreement has not yet been reached. The Parliament delegation taking part in the meeting is the delegation constituted and responsible for this particular dossier.

The dossier under discussion is handled by using the joint four-column working document prepared by the Parliament and the Council conciliation services. It is divided in two parts: Part A: Amendments on which agreement has been reached (subject to overall agreement), and Part B: Amendments on which agreement is still to be found. The discussion is normally limited to these outstanding issues. The Commission can be invited to propose compromise texts to facilitate agreement. Sometimes declarations by one or more of the institutions are also used as a tool to reach an agreement.

If an agreement seems to be within reach, the Conciliation Committee meetings are normally scheduled to start in the late afternoon or evening and can last - if necessary - several hours, even until the small hours of the morning. However, the co-chairs of the committee may decide to establish in advance the time when the meeting will be concluded. If it seems to be clear that no agreement will be found at the first meeting, any number of further meetings can be convened within the six week (or eight, if extended) deadline for reaching an agreement. If the two institutions fail to reach an agreement in the Conciliation Committee, the whole proposal falls.

Following a successful conclusion of the conciliation procedure a draft joint text, known as PE-CONS, is prepared. Once the Parliament and the Council have finalised this joint text, the co-presidents of the Conciliation Committee send it along with a transmission letter to the President of the Parliament and the President of the Council. Any declarations by the institutions are annexed to this letter. From the signature of the transmission letter approving the joint text, the two institutions have six weeks (or eight, if extended) to adopt the act, without any possibility to further amend it. The vote on the joint text is preceded by a debate in the plenary on the outcome of the negotiations and the agreement reached with the Council. The debate

Main differences
between the First/
Second reading
and Third reading
with conciliation
in parliament

FIRST AND SECOND READING	CONCILIATION (THIRD READING)
Primary responsibility lies with the parliamentary committee(s) involved	Primary responsibility lies with the EP delegation
First reading: no time limits Second reading: max. 4 months for the EP and another max. 4 months for the Council	Third reading: max. 24 weeks (3x8 weeks), of which max. 8 weeks devoted to conciliation
Possibility to table amendments in the committees and in the plenary	No amendments allowed: approval or rejection of the joint text as a whole
First reading: EP adopts amendments by simple majority Second reading: EP adopts amendments by absolute majority (at least 367 votes)	EP approves the joint text by simple majority in a single vote

in the plenary normally begins with a statement by the rapporteur (and in exceptional cases by the Vice President chairing the delegation). Parliament then votes on the joint text. A simple majority of the votes cast is required for approval. Otherwise, the joint text is rejected. The plenary normally endorses the agreement reached in the Conciliation Committee. During the last parliamentary term only 2 agreements out of 86 reached in conciliation (or 0,5% of the total) failed to find a majority in the plenary at the Third Reading.

Knowing this complex and diversified legislative procedure with its different actors is nothing less but crucial for your lobbying success. Make sure you understand it.

2.5 Other procedures

2.5.1 Simplified procedure

This procedure only applies to measures within the Commission's own powers such as approval of state aid. The simplified procedure is also used for the adoption of non-mandatory instruments, especially recommendations and opinions issued by the Commission or the Council. The Commission can also formulate recommendations and deliver opinions where it considers it necessary.

2.5.2 Procedure for implementing measures (Comitology)

Comitology

The general rule is that the Council confers on the Commission the power to issue measures implementing its instrument. Only in special cases may the Council reserve implementing powers for itself. When exercising its implementing powers, the Commission may neither amend nor supplement the Council instrument. Compliance with the framework conditions laid down by the Council is ensured through committees. The Parliament may, in these instances, deliver a reasoned opinion stating that the planned measure exceeds the scope of the legal instrument to be implemented, and may require the Commission to modify the implementing measure accordingly. In addition, the Commission is subject to wide-ranging obligations to keep the Parliament informed and properly notified. The three committee procedures, whose application is specified in the enabling instrument, are used as follows:

2.5.2.1 Advisory Committee procedure

This procedure applies chiefly to the implementation of Council instruments for the single market. The Advisory Committee is made up of representatives of the Member States and chaired by a Commission representative. The Commission representative presents a draft of the measures to be taken and the committee gives its opinion on them within a time limit set by the Commission according to the urgency of the matter. The Commission is expected, though not obliged, to take the fullest possible account of the opinion. It informs the committee of the action taken on its suggestions and proposed amendments.

2.5.2.2 Management Committee procedure

This procedure has been used for measures implementing the common agricultural policy, the common fisheries policy, or programmes

While not all of them are always part of a draft law process, these are the stages when the Commission explicitly asks the stakeholders to say what they think about a new policy proposal.

In its Consultations on the Commission website[74], the Commission addresses all stakeholders in search for information regarding certain policy areas that it intends to become active on. The Green Papers, very broadly, cover a certain policy area, disclosing the ideas and intentions the Commission has in that field, while the White Papers are already very precise and contain concrete measures the Commission intends to take. The draft laws, i.e. directives or regulations are also very detailed and, from the Commission's point of view, cover the policy issue, including stakeholders' opinions, therefore leaving only limited room for maneuver in the Commission.

How does the process unfold? After a consultation and/or a Green Paper, the Commission develops a White Paper.

COMMISSION OF THE EUROPEAN COMMUNITIES

Brussels, 27.2.2001

COM(2001) 88 final

WHITE PAPER

Strategy for a future Chemicals Policy

(presented by the Commission)

[74] http://europa.eu.int/yourvoice/consultations/index_en.htm
[75] http://ec.europa.eu/environment/chemicals/pdf/0188_en.pdf

As a response to this White Paper, the Commission usually receives comments in written and oral form from the stakeholders[76]. All this is published on the Commission website[77].

EUROPEAN COMMISSION

ENTERPRISE DIRECTORATE-GENERAL
ENVIRONMENT DIRECTORATE-GENERAL

**REACH REGULATION
PUBLIC INTERNET CONSULTATION**

A - Contact details
(Please enter your contact details)

Name: **Procter & Gamble Europe**

B - Confidentiality

☐   **I would like my identity to be kept confidential**
(please leave this box blank if you agree that your name and organisation will be identified on the Commission's website for public access)

C - SME

☐   **Are you a small or medium sized enterprise?** (EC legal definition)
please specify the number of members:

D - Description of your primary activities
(please select only one of the following)

Industry

☒   **Manufacturer**
☒   **Importer**
☒   **Downstream user**
☐   **Distributor**
☐   **Trade association**
☐   **Other**

P&G sells more than 300 consumer product brands in more than 160 countries (including the EU) such as laundry and cleaning products, cosmetic products, paper hygiene products, medical devices, drugs and food and beverages.

P&G represents in Western Europe:
- 23,000 employees
- ground operations in 16 countries
- 5 R&D centers
- Net sales of 9,075 million €

NGO

☐   **Environmental group**
☐   **Animal welfare group**
☐   **Trade union**
☐   **Consumer organisation**

Example

Responses of industry, NGOs and associations on REACH White Paper

[76] See for example http://ec.europa.eu/enterprise/reach/consultation/contributions_en.htm
[77] Regarding the REACH initiative: http://ec.europa.eu/enterprise/reach/consultation_en.htm

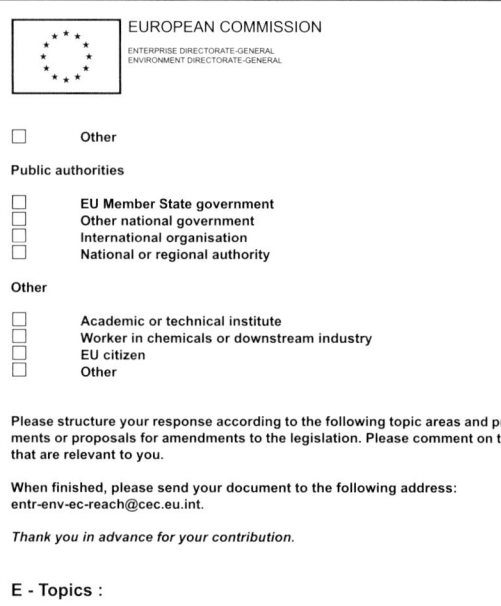

EUROPEAN COMMISSION

ENTERPRISE DIRECTORATE-GENERAL
ENVIRONMENT DIRECTORATE-GENERAL

☐   Other

Public authorities

☐   EU Member State government
☐   Other national government
☐   International organisation
☐   National or regional authority

Other

☐   Academic or technical institute
☐   Worker in chemicals or downstream industry
☐   EU citizen
☐   Other

Please structure your response according to the following topic areas and provide comments or proposals for amendments to the legislation. Please comment on those topics that are relevant to you.

When finished, please send your document to the following address:
entr-env-ec-reach@cec.eu.int.

Thank you in advance for your contribution.

E - Topics :

0. Summary – General comments

P&G supports among others the comments provided by the following trade associations or organizations; DUCC, AISE, HERA, Colipa, EDANA, ETS, Chemical Users Round Table, EC-ETOC and Amcham.

We agree with the overall objectives of the new chemical policy as described in the White Paper. However, our overall impression of the Consultation Document is that the new process looks actually more complex than the current regulations. This is not promising from a workability point of view; in particular the level of additional administrative burden entailed raises concerns.

As Procter and Gamble is a manufacturer of consumer products and thus, representative of a large downstream user, it is essential to us that:

1. Downstream users have the explicit **possibility** to engage at all stages of the REACH process, from pre-registration through to

EUROPEAN COMMISSION

ENTERPRISE DIRECTORATE-GENERAL
ENVIRONMENT DIRECTORATE-GENERAL

authorization, including aspects like public information, classification etc....

2. **Scope:** Polymers should be exempt from registration. Only substances used in articles that would be classified as dangerous according to the Dangerous Substance Directive (67/548/EEC), which are released during intended and reasonably foreseeable conditions of use (and not during disposal) and in sufficiently high amount to adversely affect human health and the environment, should be registered.
Overlap of scopes between REACH (as a whole or at some stages) and other health, environment or product legislations should be avoided.

3. **Information through the supply chain:** The proposed tool i.e. the chemical safety report, is far too complex. It should be replaced by an expanded and comprehensive safety data sheet containing only relevant information for the downstream users further down the chain i.e. the hazard information on the substances and the safe handling measures for each intended use of the substance.

4. **Downstream users responsibilities.**
Each actor in the supply chain should be able to participate to the elaboration of the chemical safety assessment with the supplier from the onset. Moreover, each actor in the supply chain should only check whether the safe handling measures, as indicated in the safety data sheet, are appropriate for his own intended use and not for the intended uses of the downstream users further down the chain.

5. **Chemical Safety Assessment:** the chemical safety assessment as proposed in the text should be simplified more in order to be workable.
The risk assessment model proposed by ECETOC may be a practical approach to accomplish this assessment.
(for more details see the following website: www.ecetoc.org)
Moreover the HERA project (Health and Environmental Risk Assessment on substances used in household cleaning products) to which we are actively contributing, is a good model of establishing a single and common Chemical Safety Assessment for substances or groups of substances through collaboration between suppliers and downstream users. This chemical safety assessment is a targeted risk assessment which is done regardless of tonnage at which chemicals are produced or imported and encompasses all available data from the onset (cf HERA website : www.heraproject.com). HERA is keen to see that risk assessments prepared under the HERA programme are recognised under REACH.

The chemical safety assessment of substances used in an article should not cover the life-cycle of the substance when it is part of an article except when it complies with the definition of "substance used in article" defined in "Section 2: Scope" above.

Following this interaction with the stakeholders, the Commission prepares its draft law on the issue, before sending it to the Parliament[78].

[78] http://europa.eu.int/eur-lex/en/com/pdf/2003/com2003_0644en.html

Example
Commission's draft
regulation and draft
directive on REACH

 COMMISSION OF THE EUROPEAN COMMUNITIES

Brussels, 29.10.2003
COM(2003) 644 final

2003/0256(COD)
2003/0257(COD)

VOLUME I

Proposal for a

REGULATION OF THE EUROPEAN PARLIAMENT AND OF THE COUNCIL

concerning the Registration, Evaluation, Authorisation and Restriction of Chemicals
(REACH), establishing a European Chemicals Agency and amending Directive
1999/45/EC and Regulation (EC) {on Persistent Organic Pollutants}

Proposal for a

DIRECTIVE OF THE EUROPEAN PARLIAMENT AND OF THE COUNCIL

amending Council Directive 67/548/EEC in order to adapt it to Regulation (EC) of
the European Parliament and of the Council concerning the registration, evaluation,
authorisation and restriction of chemicals

(presented by the Commission)
{SEC(2003 1171}

There are diverse ways for you to get into the game:

You should first try to acquire crucial positions in the decision making process such as becoming a member of a consultative committee or an expert group established by the Commission. Since the Commission totters almost permanently on the brink of both volume and content overload, it has to rely on various techniques to manage day-to-day business. On the one hand, the Commission therefore tries to reduce the overload, for example, by selecting priorities, combining issues and phasing policies. On the other hand the Commission tries to expand its capacities in two ways. Firstly, by the outsourcing of work particularly to national governments (implementation and inspection), which is part of the subsidiary principle, and to private consultancies (research). Secondly, by bringing in external expertise, especially lobbyists, who thereby get an open door for their provision of sectoral information and who are invited to participate in the relevant committees, to provide for the Commission's assistance bureaucracy[79]. The first category of these committees are the so-called expert groups, having semi-formal advisory status without any formal powers, being composed of experts from public or private interest groups. The number of expert groups amounts to 1,000-2,000, not all of them being registered. About 50,000 people meet in the registered groups and these are drawn from the Member States lobbying groups. Meeting about 10 days a year they are an impressive additional workforce for the Commission. The second category of committees comprises the around 450 so-called comitology groups, mentioned above in the legislative procedures. They are constituted of people officially representing the Member States, are practically run by the Commission and do have formal powers ranging from advisory and management to regulatory.

Tip

Try to become a member of one of the external committees that consult the Commission

The Commission has set up a public register of the expert groups that help it in preparing legislative proposals and policy initiatives[80]. The register covers formal and informal advisory bodies. It provides information on the nature and tasks of each group, and indicates which department within the Commission is responsible for overseeing which group. Through these committees the Commission is often able to call on external specialists to help often very diverse and technical areas from the setting of targets for air quality, to authorising cosmetic products, establishing automobile safety standards, determining sustainable fish catches, developing strategies to tackle unemployment or public health concerns, or designing European research programmes. The register provides an overview of the groups that help the Commission and provides information on the groups' tasks, the lead service in the Commission and the general composition of the group. It covers a total of around 1,300 expert groups.

Secondly, you should try to acquire positions in the relevant committees of other stakeholders – often associations - lobbying the Commission, for example associations like AmCham EU. If you lobby for a pharmaceutical company, try to head the respective committees in the relevant associations and become a member of committees neighbouring that policy area. That puts you in the position to draft the official statement of that association, reflecting your own stakeholder's political position to a large extent. Thereby you can advocate your own

[79] van Schendelen, Machiavelli in Brussels, p. 67
[80] http://ec.europa.eu/secretariat_general/regexp/

political opinion through diverse channels and give it a broader base.

When lobbying the Commission, you can lobby the relevant DG "bottom-up". That means you can address your activity to those officials who write the particular draft proposal, since experts and officials at a lower level draft most legislation. The chef de dossier makes the first draft or receives this from the outside, i.e. the expert committees. The Head of Unit usually sets only the objectives, checks the draft texts and, if required, pushes for approval at political level of the Commission, such as the Commissioner, his Cabinet or the College[81].

Since most officials first rely on the information they receive from their staff, it is as important to seek to influence the staff as it is to lobby the decision maker himself[82].

In many cases, these staff members are a main starting point since, after their drafting, any modification to the original text will be difficult. Long-term relationships of lobbyists in the market are an asset in such case. Regardless of the neutrality of Commission officials, one should not underestimate personal relationships: As an official,

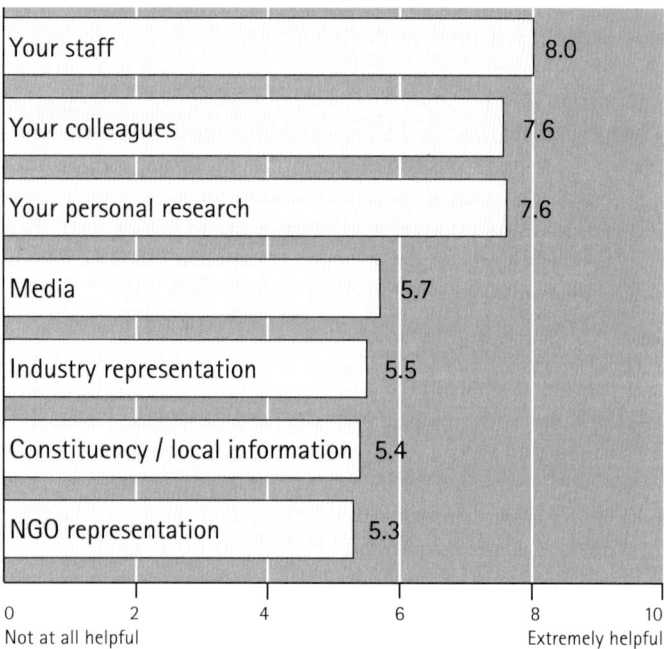

Helpfulness of different information sources

Your staff	8.0
Your colleagues	7.6
Your personal research	7.6
Media	5.7
Industry representation	5.5
Constituency / local information	5.4
NGO representation	5.3

0   2   4   6   8   10
Not at all helpful   Extremely helpful

(?) Please rate the following sources in terms of how helpful each one is in providing you with what you need to make informed decisions in your work.

[81] van Schendelen, Machiavelli in Brussels, p. 95
[82] Burson-Marsteller, The Definitive Guide to Lobbying the European Institutions, p. 12

you need to know whose information you can trust. If a lobbyist is well known and respected or even has friends in that DG drafting the particular directive or regulation, he might have a good chance of getting his voice heard and his arguments through. It is like everything in life: If you share values, interests or even nationality, this can constitute an advantage, though it does not necessarily have to.

You can also lobby the Commission "top down" by turning attention and efforts directly to the Commissioner, his cabinet, or to the Director General in charge. The top levels can, of course, influence the mid- and lower levels. But they usually do so in the early phases of agenda-making, when the paper on the desk is still blank. However, talking to the Director General can be a good idea if you have direct access. But it can also be counterproductive, since you might end up, again, presenting your arguments to the offical that is drafting the law. He might feel overrun by you turning to his boss instead of turning to him. Lobbying the Commissioner in charge, however, is mostly a lobbying style less based exclusively on facts, but instead of a more political nature and argumenting. Consequently, you need a very good, high-ranking political network to gain such access. And you need convincing political arguments. In addition, if a political initiative has strong implications for certain Member States it might make sense not only to talk to the Commissioner in charge of the matter but to the Commissioners from the Member States concerned the most. You can try to convince these Commissioners to discuss the relevant arguments in the College. You stand a good chance because, regardless of the national neutrality of the Commissioners, they are still politically appointed by their Member States and have an eye on the political implications of a policy initiative.

3.1.2 Administrative Lobbying

As discussed, the Commission has not only a legislative but also an administrative function regarding the implementation of EU policies. One of the most important administrative functions is probably the implementation of EU competition policy. The merger and cartel decisions of the Commission affect industry and the corporate world on a worldwide scale. A merger that has not been cleared in Brussels cannot be executed anywhere else in the world either. A company that has been found to violate EU cartel rules can be fined by Brussels – even if it sits in Ohio. Unsurprisingly, it has been this function of the Commission that has primarily led US enterprises to the decision to lobby in Brussels as they do in Washington.

Tip

If you lobby based on technical facts and data, lobby "bottom up", i.e. the lower ranking officials and the staff members first. If you lobby based on political arguments, lobby "top down"

Example
Commission's
merger decision on
GE/Honeywell

This text is made available for information purposes only and does not constitute an official publication.
The official text of the decision will be published in the Official Journal of the European Communities

Commission Decision

of 03/07/2001

declaring a concentration to be incompatible with the common market

and the EEA Agreement

Case No COMP/M.2220 – General Electric/Honeywell

(Only the English text is authentic)

(Text with EEA relevance)

THE COMMISSION OF THE EUROPEAN COMMUNITIES,

Having regard to the Treaty establishing the European Community,

Having regard to the Agreement on the European Economic Area, and in particular Article 57 thereof,

Having regard to Council Regulation (EEC) No 4064/89 of 21 December 1989 on the control of concentrations between undertakings[1], as last amended by Regulation (EC) No 1310/97[2], and in particular Article 8(3) thereof,

Having regard to the Commission's decision of 1 March 2001 to initiate proceedings in this case,

---

[1] OJ L 395, 30.12.1989, p. 1; corrected version OJ L 257, 21.9.1990, p. 13

[2] OJ L 180, 9.7.1997, p. 1.

The major difference compared to legislative lobbying is that, in administrative cases, only the Commission, and no other EU institution, is involved. Secondly, there are fewer stakeholders in these cases since usually there are only a handful of companies affected by an administrative decision of the Commission, while on the other hand a draft law affects a whole industry.

When lobbying in administrative cases - whether this is about getting through (or hampering) a merger, filing a complaint against a competitor for abuse of his dominant market position or defending your stakeholder's position with regard to an alleged cartel - your job is, more than anything, about convincing the Commission case handler from your legal point of view. The possibilities of lobbying "bottom up" or "top down" are much more limited even though in larger competition cases the Commissioner for Competition has been targeted several times in the past directly.

When you lobby competition issues, it helps to be a lawyer: Most of those administrative decisions are afterwards being challenged in the European Court of Justice anyhow. Therefore, a major focus is on legal arguments in those cases. PR or political arguments do not fly nearly as well.

Since you need an attorney to take the case to the European Court of Justice, much of the Commission lobbying is done by the competition lawyers from major US or UK law firms mainly, like Cleary or Linklaters. After the Commission decided to follow a more economic and less legal approach when deciding on competition issues, economic consultancies like Charles River Associates or NERA have also stepped into the ring.

TRIBUNAL DE PRIMERA INSTANCIA DE LAS COMUNIDADES EUROPEAS
SOUD PRVNÍHO STUPNĚ EVROPSKÝCH SPOLEČENSTVÍ
DE EUROPÆISKE FÆLLESSKABERS RET I FØRSTE INSTANS
GERICHT ERSTER INSTANZ DER EUROPÄISCHEN GEMEINSCHAFTEN
EUROOPA ÜHENDUSTE ESIMESE ASTME KOHUS
ΠΡΩΤΟΔΙΚΕΙΟ ΤΩΝ ΕΥΡΩΠΑΪΚΩΝ ΚΟΙΝΟΤΗΤΩΝ
COURT OF FIRST INSTANCE OF THE EUROPEAN COMMUNITIES
TRIBUNAL DE PREMIÈRE INSTANCE DES COMMUNAUTÉS EUROPÉENNES
CÚIRT CHÉADCHÉIME NA gCOMHPHOBAL EORPACH
TRIBUNALE DI PRIMO GRADO DELLE COMUNITÀ EUROPEE
EIROPAS KOPIENU PIRMĀS INSTANCES TIESA

EUROPOS BENDRIJŲ PIRMOSIOS INSTANCIJOS TEISMAS
EURÓPAI KÖZÖSSÉGEK ELSŐFOKÚ BÍRÓSÁGA
IL-QORTI TAL-PRIM ISTANZA TAL-KOMUNITAJIET EWROPEJ
GERECHT VAN EERSTE AANLEG VAN DE EUROPESE GEMEENSCHAPPEN
SĄD PIERWSZEJ INSTANCJI WSPÓLNOT EUROPEJSKICH
TRIBUNAL DE PRIMEIRA INSTÂNCIA DAS COMUNIDADES EUROPEIAS
SÚD PRVÉHO STUPŇA EURÓPSKYCH SPOLOČENSTIEV
SODIŠČE PRVE STOPNJE EVROPSKIH SKUPNOSTI
EUROOPAN YHTEISÖJEN ENSIMMÄISEN OIKEUSASTEEN TUOMIOISTUIN
EUROPEISKA GEMENSKAPERNAS FÖRSTAINSTANSRÄTT

Press and Information

PRESS RELEASE No° 109/05

14 December 2005

Judgment of the Court of First Instance in Cases T-209/01 and T-210/01

Honeywell v Commission and General Electric v Commission

THE COURT OF FIRST INSTANCE UPHOLDS THE PROHIBITION OF GENERAL ELECTRIC'S ACQUISITION OF HONEYWELL

Although the Commission made errors in its decision declaring the concentration to be incompatible with the common market, in particular in its analysis of conglomerate effects resulting from the concentration, the fact that dominant positions would have been created or strengthened on several specific product markets is sufficient to justify that decision

On 5 February 2001, the European Commission received notification of a merger between the United States companies Honeywell International and General Electric Company ("GE"). By decision of 3 July 2001, the Commission declared the merger incompatible with the common market and, consequently, the parties were prohibited from putting the merger into effect in the European Union.

GE and Honeywell brought actions before the Court of First Instance for annulment of that decision. The British company, Rolls-Royce, and the United States company, Rockwell Collins, intervened in both cases in support of the European Commission.

The Court has approved the Commission's findings that the merger would create or strengthen dominant positions as a result of which effective competition would be significantly impeded on three markets:

– the market for jet engines for large regional aircraft;

– the market for engines for corporate jet aircraft;

– the market for small marine gas turbines.

Those findings are sufficient for it to be concluded that the merger is incompatible with the common market. The Court has not therefore annulled the decision, even though the Commission made errors in relation to other aspects of the case, in particular in its analysis of conglomerate effects.

Example

European Court of Justice merger decision on GE/Honeywell

However, even while the focus in these cases is rather based on hard facts than on PR, due to some unwelcome and difficult merger decisions like the GE/Honeywell and the Tetra Laval cases, both law firms and economic consultancies got into discussions whether they might have shown a lack of "merger communication" in the past, i.e. not communicating their facts and arguments accordingly well enough via the decision makers. The same is true for the respective "cartel communication", giving companies being accused of creating a cartel or abusing their dominant market position - like Microsoft lately - a hard time in Brussels. For most consultancies, this has led to a change in strategy in the last few years, either trying to combine their competencies with external PR agencies or hiring their own in-house PR consultants.

3.2 The European Parliament

In its legislative function, the Parliament is a prime target for lobby-ists'. Since Parliament does not legislate autonomously, but decides based on the proposals drafted by the Commission and approved later on by the Council, in all the cases where legislative power is shared between the Council and the Parliament under co-decision, lobbying the Parliament is crucial.

If you did not get through your opinion in the Commission or if you are too late for that since the draft is already out, head for the Parliament. The same is true if you do not want to influence but to initiate a legislative draft from a certain (national) business perspective. The Parliament has also constituted in the past a point of reference for many smaller groups, which may not have enjoyed such an easy access to the Commission or national governments in the lobbying process.

Lobbying the Parliament usually starts when the rapporteur, who is the member of the parliamentary committee in charge, responsible

Start with the
EP rapporteur

for examining a new draft law and reporting on it, begins to write the report for the First Reading of the Parliament - and before the committee and party groups start discussing it. He is the one who will have the most knowledge about the subject in question being able to pick up and judge lobbyists arguments. This is the reason why the most important people to lobby are the rapporteur or the so-called shadow rapporteurs, i.e. the Parliamentarians being appointed by their respective groups to deal with the Commission draft, as explained above. The other members of the committee in charge will usually have no chance to deal with the issue in detail. The resources of all MEPs to cope with the information load – time and staff – are very limited. Since you are lobbying the "working level" here, it can also be helpful in this case to contact the assistants, i.e. professional staff members, of the MEPs. They are the ones dealing with the calendar, mail and email of the MEPs – and thereby filtering the information. Another important address to lobby is the chairman of the Parliament committee that examines the Commission draft. For example, if the Commission draft is about energy issues, you can be sure that the respective committee in the Parliament will take care of it. Given the relevance of these committees described above, you can even beforehand try to influence the appointment of certain MEPs as rapporteurs on subjects in which you regard them as helpful. Further, since they offer the opportunity to hear experts, special standing committees are more accessible to lobbyists than the plenary session and they represent a good place to convince MEPs to amend the legislative text under review. You can also try addressing leaders of party groups so that they give voting instructions to their colleagues both within the committees and the assembly[83].

In the Second Reading of the Parliament, the rapporteur is still the primary address point for lobbying. However, if there is a tendency that certain parliamentary fractions or groups of MEPs intend to introduce amendments in the decision making process, it is also useful to lobby the corresponding fraction leader, the committee coordinator of that fraction or its speaker.

If a draft law is sent to the Conciliation Committee, however, the lobbying focus changes: Three Vice Presidents of the Parliament, the Chair of the competent committee and the rapporteur, as well as the other members of the Conciliation Committee are potential targets for your lobbying efforts now.

In the Third Reading, however, there is not much use lobbying the Parliament. Changes in the draft law by Parliament are not possible anymore.

When lobbying the Parliament you should also be aware of two things.

First, the most important thing for an MEP is to be reelected. For most MEPs their mandate is equivalent to their sheer economic existence. Many stakeholders wonder why an MEP did not understand their arguments and did not follow them in voting, even though these ar-

Tip

When meeting with an MEP,

- know his constituencies
- know his biography
- know where he comes from geographically and personally
- know his political ambitions, network, friends and enemies
- ask yourself, what influence does he have on his party, committee, the public etc.
- ask yourself, what moves him and whether what you want from him also promotes and helps his interests – or quite the opposite

This kind of personal data about the politicians is available on commercial political databases such as www.europeanagenda.eu

[83] Marziali, Lobbying in Brussels, p. 21

Example
Parliament's
amendments
on Commission's
REACH draft laws[84]

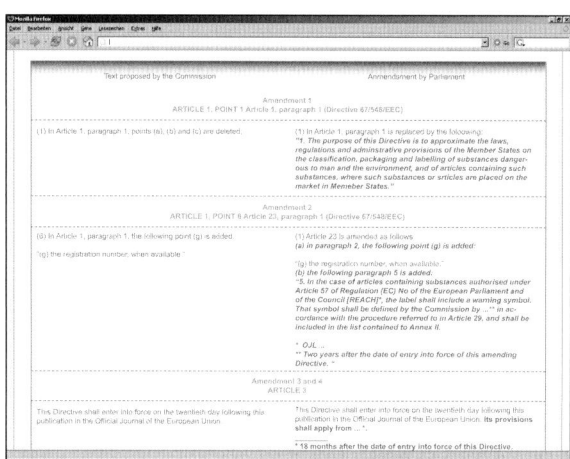

guments are quite obvious and easy to comprehend. The answer is: he probably understood you, and perhaps he even thinks you are right. But he knows that if he supported this kind of politics he would lose the support of his voters at home. And this fact is more important to him. Therefore, to get him vote in favour of your arguments and perhaps even gain him as a supporter speaking up for your ideas, you have to create a situation that makes it politically possible for him. You have to create a win-win-situation for the MEP, explaining why your position favours his own political interests.

The second thing you need to be aware of is that, even though EU lobbying in general is not so much different from lobbying in other parts of the world, e.g. Washington, many US companies experienced that there is a difference between parliamentary lobbying in Brussels and in Washington. The reason is basically that the electoral campaigns are so different on the two sides of the Atlantic. In the US, candidates who decide to stand election must seek political support and money, as there is no party discipline or candidature control. In the EU, on the other hand, national issues and national parties dominate electoral campaigns for the Parliament elections and MEPs look for votes in their constituencies. In other words, whereas the US Members of Congress consider corporations as their electorate which finance election campaigns through so called Political Action Committees (PACs), European election financing is completely different, which is why MEPs see their constituency represented by the voters and not by interest groups. You should therefore adapt your lobbying style accordingly in Brussels: show some respect.

[84] http://www.europarl.europa.eu

3.3 The Council of the European Union

There are several ways to ensure that your views are represented in the Council meetings. These ways are complementary and do not exclude each other.

You can either lobby the national representatives or the home governments in their Member States. But be aware that lobbying the Council goes beyond the attempt to influence the positions by national governments only. This might make sense if unanimity in the Council is required. In such cases, sometimes it even makes sense to concentrate all lobbying efforts on a veto from a certain government and not waste lobbying resources on Parliament and Commission. Nevertheless, usually in order to form the necessary coalitions in the Council either to pass a proposal or to block it, a lobbyist also needs to turn to other governments.

You can also lobby the staff of the Council and the civil servants of the Council's Secretariat General. Since everything is already decided when ministers are called to vote, you have to intervene in the earliest phases of the examination of a directive or a regulation by the Council.

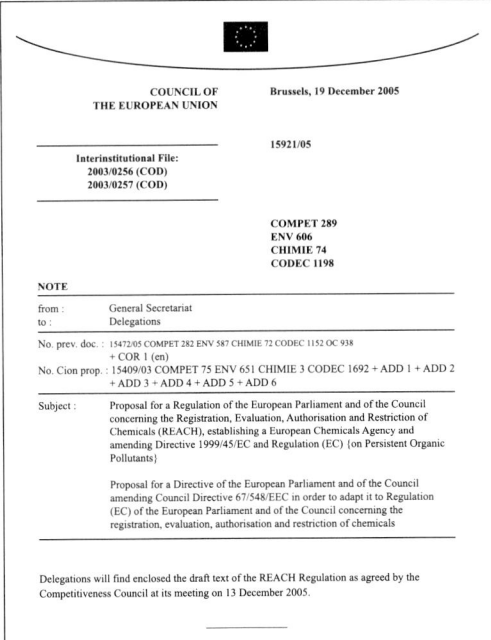

Example

Council adoption of REACH proposal[87]

⁸⁷ http://register.consilium.eu.int/pdf/en/05/st15/st15921.en05.pdf

This is the reason why you should lobby the Permanent Representations to the EU. Here you find the diplomats that serve their governments as members of the Coreper and the civil servants that participate in the Council working groups and prepare the ground for meetings of Coreper and ministerial Councils.

You should also target the staff of each presidency. Since the government that holds the 6-month presidency of the Council is responsible for setting the political agenda, it is fundamental for every lobbyist to address his lobbying towards the Permanent Representation of the one country that holds the presidency[85].

But among the most relevant actors for you to lobby are those who determine the Council position: the mainly national civil servants sitting in the working groups under Coreper and in the special committees. They make the bulk of the decisions, which are rubberstamped by the ministers. They are all appointed nationally and they can be influenced in their Member States[86].

3.4 The Member States' governments and parliaments

As mentioned, Member States' governments fulfil an important function with regard to the Council. Small companies or interest groups, which have insufficient resources and staff to lobby or even to open an office in Brussels, find this national route, which takes place in the respective capitals, easier. Moreover, one should not forget that national governments respond directly to their parliaments and to their electors regarding the positions taken within the Council: they gain politically from sponsoring domestic interest groups, as the latter in the future will be grateful to the government in terms of political support.

However, those national governments have another function which makes it important to keep them on your EU lobbying agenda. When looking at the implementation of directives into Member States' laws it becomes obvious that a lobbyist cannot restrict himself to lobbying the EU institutions only or even to separate EU lobbying from national lobbying. As discussed, directives only provide for a frame law, which has to be filled in by the national legislator through a national law and this usually provides for a certain bandwidth that the national legislator can exercise. This means that you get a second shot: The same arguments you have made in Brussels can now be put forward in national capitals.

[85] Marziali, Lobbying in Brussels, p. 17
[86] van Schendelen, Machiavelli in Brussels, p. 96

Furthermore, your stakeholder's interests do not necessarily need to be identical in all Member States. While your stakeholder, as a global player, might have some local competitor in France, he may have no such competitor in the UK. Therefore, no matter what you achieved on the EU level as directive bandwidth, you still might be forced to act in the implementation phase of that directive on the Member State level anyhow. While a certain emission benchmark of an environment directive being implemented in the UK might not disturb you, in France the same benchmark might put your stakeholder under pressure for giving his competitor a competitive advantage in the market. So in the same case you might need to aim for different implementation solutions of the same directive and therefore argue differently when talking to different national governments and parliaments.

Your targets in the Member States are, of course, the respective case handlers in the national ministries of the Member States' governments in charge of the implementation of the directive. But your targets are also the national parliamentarians, since they have to vote on the new national law implementing the directive in the end. Lobbying the national parliaments, of course, has to take into consideration the different national characteristics and peculiarities. But, in principle, it follows the same rule as lobbying the MEPs: focus on the rapporteurs, the respective committees and the party leaders.

However, there is no way for you to keep up good personal contacts and relationships with all the players in the different Member States' capitals yourself. This is why you need to have a lobbying network in the Member States. While, of course, you should be in control of the lobbying initiative on an EU wide scale to avoid diverging or contradictory lobbying on the local spot, you need to have some people on the ground in Berlin, London, Paris etc. to stay in touch with the local decision makers.

Tip

Lobby the Council
- in Brussels (Coreper and Permanent Representatives)
- in the Member State capitals (national ministers and staff)

4. Lobbying tools

How does a lobbyist best get his message over to the one he lobbies? And how does he best ensure that his position cannot be neglected by the decision makers? Here are your tools:

4.1 Monitoring

Stay informed Information is the currency a lobbyist deals with. Being well informed about what is going on is the basis of all lobbying. Only if you have the necessary piece of information before others do, will you survive in the long run. Monitoring is the instrument that helps you to be informed. Monitoring has another task. It is also the basis for you to know when to intervene in which way. It ensures your participation in the legislative process and therefore is the first step in each lobbyist's decision making process.

Monitoring can be compared to a radar system. In fact, it is an early warning system. Things in Brussels will not happen without you knowing about them. Like on a radar screen, the lobbyist filters signals from the air and ensures that his stakeholder is informed about EU issues that are of interest for him at an early stage. Ideally, the lobbyists covers such issues before they become part of the daily news.

Monitoring, therefore, basically means information gathering. That includes going through agendas and finding what is relevant for your purposes. On a more sophisticated level, it can involve any number of methods for obtaining political intelligence.

Your first starting point are the websites of the EU institutions, where the legislative initiatives are announced:

On the Commission website (http://ec.europa.eu/index_en.htm) you will find the different policy areas of the EU and the latest information about legislation in each area, including recent press announcements of the respective directorates in charge.

You will find more detailed information about ongoing legislative procedures and the process stage of each draft law on the Legislative Observatory (Oeil) website of the Parliament (www.europarl.europa.eu/oeil/).

The next step is the Commission website on which the current policy consultations are published (http://europa.eu.int/yourvoice/consultations/index_en.htm), so you know what policy initiatives there are. This is complemented by the website on which the statements made to those consultations by the interested parties (lobbyists) are being presented[88].

Besides that, probably the best source for publicly available information is still the daily bulletin from Agence Europe (www.agenceurope.com). Large parts of the EU monitoring service industry draw their information from here and put it into their newsletters. Therefore, you may as well buy the original source directly instead of paying them for it.

But a good lobbyist cannot depend on publicly available information only. You need a network of contacts and informal conversation to get hold of the issue – and the written draft - before it becomes public. There is a reason why Brussels' most successful lobbyists are the ones who have been around for some time and are permanent players in the political scene. If you stick around, you get to know people, and if you know people, you have not only greater opportunity for influence, but also know where to go to get in on the action. Forget about fly-in-fly-out. Year after year, more firms, industries and associations are coming to Brussels realising that, in order to have a seat at the table, you at least need to be in the dining room.

4.2 Identification and Analysis

This is not only about analysing current and potential consequences of EU law. It is also about analysing your stakeholder. You should devote sufficient time and attention to the stakeholder you lobby for and the business problems he has or might have. What are his interests, what is his business, what does he do? And what is his strategy, what does he want? Not all aspects of his activities being potentially affected by changes in EU law are visible at a first glance. And, in the end, there might be a lot more Commission DGs involved than you first thought.

Does your stakeholder produce washing powder? Then this of course involves chemicals. And environment. And consumer protection? Competition and internal market issues affect almost every business, too. And what about the upstream, downstream and other markets? Does your stakeholder have to care about the latest draft law from DG Energy affecting producers of washing machines? And does he really only produce washing powder? Unilever, for instance, recently found that it had 1,600 separate products and therefore 29 separate EU trade association affiliations[89].

Tip
The broader your monitoring tools are, of course, the bigger are your chances not to miss anything important. Broad press coverage is therefore quite important. But your monitoring sources should at least include:

- Agence Europe
- The Financial Times
- EU institutions' websites
- Speeches of officials
- Position and draft papers
- Personal network and contacts

[88] http://prelex.europa.eu
[89] Greenwood, Interest representation in the European Union, p. 26

Of course, no stakeholder can cover every little subject and it would be wrong to split your resources to many different areas instead of focusing them on the most important ones. But you need to make sure you know what happens in the areas that concern you and that at least someone else is covering the issues you cannot cover yourself. As a corporation, this could be your business association, a consultancy – or even your competitor. As an association or NGO, this could be your roof organisation or a neighbouring organisation with similar interests.

Analysis means that, on the basis of your monitoring, you prepare a list of priority issues your stakeholder has. Concentrate on issues that have the highest chance of occurring, particularly in the near future. Focus on issues that have strategic importance and the greatest impact on your stakeholder activities in terms of profit, costs and reputation. Choose issues that you really can do something about. Once such prime issues have been identified, a strategy has to be formulated. A blend of professional judgment, practical experience and research competence is needed for a clear understanding of an issue and the appropriate response to it. This also requires an analysis of the nature of an issue, its life cycle stage, identification of the political participants, importance of public opinion, amount and kind of media coverage and its legal regulatory and constitutional context[90]. This analysis will suggest whether your stakeholder should contain or resolve an emerging issue, or rather become active and influence public and decision makers' opinion before others do - following the reasoning that once opinions are crystallised, they are difficult to change.

Part of this analysis process, i.e. the process of finding out if and what problem your stakeholder has with a new EU policy, is that you communicate the information you gained from your monitoring into your stakeholder's organisation. Put it in a paper or newsletter update and address the respective departments in your company headquarters, the members of the association you lobby for etc. It is with your stakeholder that the technical information, expert knowledge etc. sits. Your job is not about knowing your stakeholder's problems with certain regulations in detail. No one expects you to have that technical knowledge. Your job is to have the technicians, the economists and all the other professionals from inside your stakeholder tell you their thoughts and concerns about the EU draft law. This is the information which, again, you need to collect, filter, concentrate, sum up and communicate to the EU decision makers (see "Communication" later on).

This should happen on a permanent basis and the informed people at your stakeholder should always be the same (e.g. heads of departments) so they know what to do with the information you send them.

⁹⁰ Lerbinger, Corporate Public Affairs, p. 20

4.3 Coalition building

Also, lobbying is not about being the strongest player in the arena, but about having the most allies. Therefore, build alliances and coalitions with others to pursue your goal. For a corporation, this is not the same thing as having your business association do the job for you. An old labour union saying goes: "Make no permanent friends or enemies". You will find allies in your business associations on certain issues, of course, when the interests of your whole sector are at stake. But you will as well find as many opponents in your association on all other issues since most of your competitors are to be found here, also. On the other hand, there might be many supporters of your position on a certain policy issue, which are not necessarily a member of the same associations as you are. So, regardless of Brent Spar, it may well be that, on a certain EU matter, Greenpeace is the best potential ally of Shell. Never exclude the possibility. You therefore have to actively search for your allies in the market on each different subject to build strong coalitions giving your voice a weight in the EU institutions. When looking for potential allies you have to look for their individual weaknesses and strengths to see how best to make use of them for your position.

Size is an important variable with regard to the lobby activities of your allies. Whereas large players have enough resources to undertake individual lobbying, smaller actors often have to rely on collective action to be able to undertake political action at different levels in the EU multilevel system. A second major factor that determines the organisational structure of lobby operations is economic strategy. The different market strategies of national niche players and large internationally oriented firms require different political strategies. The domestic institutional environment of the stakeholder is the third most important variable to study in order to understand the national and European lobbying activities' potential allies.

As mentioned in the beginning, different players have a different standing with the EU institutions regarding different policy issues and their respective input to it. When looking for allies and asking who could perhaps transport certain information better than you or your stakeholder can, keep in mind the different levels of lobbyist acceptance: company input is primarily respected with regard to technical and expert knowledge, while associations are seen more as general EU market information providers or national market information providers and the standing of consultants depends on the client they represent.

Tip

- Have a reservoir of contacts. Make contacts when you do not need them. Policy issues that seemed irrelevant to you yesterday might be in the center of your focus tomorrow. Potential contacts, which you therefore regarded useless and did not invest in, might be the ones you now would need most

- Determine the strategic action of the coalition members. Who does what?

- To ensure a common positioning and continuous data flow have regular meetings and common committees of the coalition members on the issues

◀

Tip

Put down the date and event on the business cards you receive, perhaps even a few keywords giving you an idea about the themes and subjects to talk about with the persons when meeting them again

Write down what interests and professional specialties the cardholders have, if possible find out their birthday date later on and contact them accordingly

Put them on your Christmas list and send them a small Christmas present.

It is important to keep your network up to date. People come and go, and you need to know where they are and what they are doing, so you can make use of them in your coalition building. Keep your database updated. Give it priorities and subjects, creating categories under which you can fit the contacts you made. If possible, use a professional IT database management system in the long run. Otherwise you will surely lose oversight.

4.4 Communication

As already mentioned, communication here works in two directions. You first have to communicate the monitoring information you gained to your stakeholder (by newsletter etc.) and receive from him the technical and market information you need to communicate back to the decision makers. To insure proper information flow between you and the experts of your stakeholder's organisation you need an established communication procedure (e.g. lobbyist – heads of departments – technicians – heads of departments – lobbyist). This is necessary to ensure you receive all available stakeholder knowledge on a certain issue, and you receive it in time. Once you have figured out what concerns your stakeholder - how can you best communicate the information you want to transport to the legislator? It is not about what you prefer. It is about what your targets prefer.

For an EU decision maker, a face-to-face meeting is the most important way in which he can receive information. Commission officials usually are the most enthusiastic for a meeting to secure information, followed by MEPs and Council officials. While written briefing material is of secondary importance to a meeting for all decision makers, Commission officials, again, are most enthusiastic

Ranking of lobbyists' information capacities

Individual Company	Expert knowledge → National information → European information
European association	European information → Expert knowledge → National information
National association	National information → Expert knowledge → European information
Consultant client=individual company	Expert knowledge → National information → European information
Consultant client=European association	European information → Expert knowledge → National information
Consultant client=National association	National information → Expert knowledge → European information

for it, followed once more by the MEPs and Council officials. When it comes to picking up the phone to transmit information, the Commission officials will be happiest to listen. Dinner or lunch briefings rate below average among decision makers as a vehicle for communicating information. In short, these events are more than half way down the list of importance: receptions are for social contact and interaction, essential in any polity or community. Meetings, written briefings, conferences, seminars, workshops and site visits are for work – and are all at the top of the ranking[91].

4.4.1 Paperwork
Consultation Papers, Green and White Papers are merely proposals and, even with draft directives and regulations, the EU institutions expect that there will be some improvement as the ideas are submitted to public scrutiny. So send them your proposals and ideas.

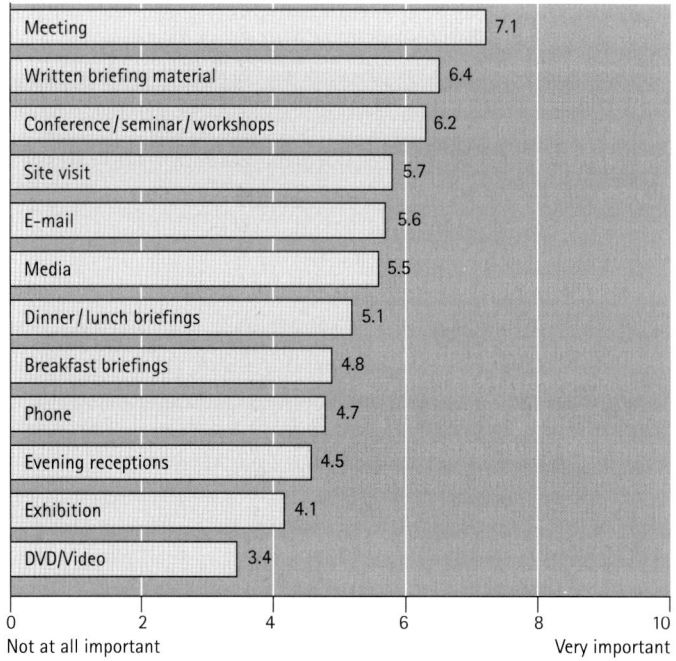

How is information best communicated?

Please rate each of the following on their level of importance in receiving information.

⁹¹ Burson-Marsteller, The Definitive Guide to Lobbying the European Institutions, p. 14

4.4.1.1 Policy papers

As discussed, there are certain kinds of information the EU institutions always need and demand from the lobbying market in the legislative process: expert knowledge, business and social information on
the European level, business and social information on the national
Member States level[92]. Therefore, this is what you have to provide for
in the policy papers and statements you send them. And comparable
to the situation that different stakeholders have a different standing
providing these types of information, the EU institutions have a different kind of interest of being provided with it[93]. So you should pay
attention to the following:

Expert knowledge is the expertise and technical know-how required
by the EU from the private sector to understand the market. In other
words, the EU institutions need precise information on the relevant
products concerned by new EU legislation to develop effective laws
in a particular policy area.

Example for technical market information:
The technical expertise provided by Deutsche Bank to help EU officials understand the particularities of the capital adequacy rules for commercial banks.
As far as information on the European level is concerned, it is necessary to
identify common EU interests, mostly regarding the aggregated needs of a
sector in the internal market. European information is often delivered by
a European business association that is spokesperson of the interests of a
particular sector at the European level.

Example for European market information:
The information provided by the European Banking Federation (FBE) on
the interests of its members with regard to the capital adequacy rules for
commercial banks.

Finally, the last kind of information concerns the national, aggregated needs and interests of sectors in the domestic markets of the
Member States.

Example for national market information:
The information provided by the German and the French banking federations respectively on the interests of their national federation members
with regard to the capital adequacy rules for commercial banks.

---

[92] Bouwen, A comparative study of business lobbying in the European Parliament, the European Commission and the Council of Ministers, p. 8
[93] Bouwen, A comparative study of business lobbying in the European Parliament, the European Commission and the Council of Ministers, p. 14

The Commission is considered the most supranational institution in the EU decision making process. It is geared towards promoting common European interests, as well as promoting its own position. The Commission is geared towards promotional brokerage, trying to push the Member States to accept policies that go beyond a purely inter governmental consensus based on the lowest common denominator. To play its role as promotional broker in the EU legislative process, the Commission needs European information.

The Commission has a substantial interest in this because it can help to identify common European interests. But since the Commission's right of legislative initiative and the related drafting of legal proposals take place in the first phase of the policy-making process and, therefore, require a substantial amount of expertise, expert knowledge is the critical resource for the Commission's legislative work. Because of under-staffing and severe budget constraints in the Commission, the institution is dependent on external resources to obtain the necessary expertise. In the agenda-setting and policy development phase, the Commission is not interested in national issues. At this early stage of the legislative process, the domestic private interests and the interests of most Member States in the issues at hand have not been identified yet. This applies even more so where technical subject matters are concerned. Besides, as promotional broker, the Commission is geared towards promoting common European interests. The institution is therefore not primarily interested in national information at all. The Commission is, however, interested in this kind of information on an ad hoc basis, when it has, for example, to amend its legislative proposal to achieve a compromise in the Council and the Parliament. National information about a particular Member State might in this case be crucial.

The Parliament, as a forum for discussions of political importance during the legislative process, has both supranational and intergovernmental characteristics. Although supranational political parties have been established in the Parliament over time, nationality remains a relevant cleavage within the assembly.

In view of the Parliament's legislative role, its demand for expert knowledge is rather limited. At this stage of the legislative process, the Commission has already drafted a detailed and often technical proposal. Although some basic expert knowledge is indispensable, the amount of technical market expertise needed to amend and take decisions is much lower in the Parliament. The Parliament particularly needs information that allows it to assess the legislative propos-

Tip
Always think about which player best delivers which kind of information and act accordingly:
• Technical and expert knowledge
• European market information
• National market information
Furthermore, all information, which you deliver, must be:
• Short
• To the point
• Easily comprehensible
• Rich in content

Tip
Commission's needs are:
Expert knowledge >
European information >
National information

Tip
Parliament's needs are:
European information >
National information >
Expert knowledge

als made by the Commission. Being directly elected by the people, the Parliament's task is to evaluate the legislative proposals from a European perspective. The specific information the Parliament requires for this assessment is therefore European information. This constitutes the institution's critical resource because it provides encompassing private-sector information about the needs and interests in the EU. In order to understand the Parliament's role in the legislative process, the constituency orientation of the MEPs has also to be taken into account. All MEPs are in fact elected at the national level and therefore retain important links with their electorate back home. In order to increase their chances for re-election, MEPs need information about their national electorate. This is why MEPs want relevant national information also. This provides them with information about the needs and preferences of their voters.

◀

Tip

Council's needs are:

National information >

European information >

Expert knowledge

The Council is the most intergovernmental institution in the EU's legislative procedures. The influence of national interests prevails in the Council and it is therefore crucial for the Council members to identify their national or domestic interest.

The Council retains a very strong demand for national information. When it comes to decision making in the Council, the proposal has already been technically elaborated and the demand for expert knowledge is therefore substantially reduced. To comment on or amend a proposal, a different kind of information is required than that required for the actual drafting by the Commission. At this stage of the decision making process, the Council is more interested in information that can facilitate the bargaining process among the Member States.

In sum, which are the critical resources of each institution? Expert knowledge for the Commission, European information for the Parliament and national information for the Council can be of some guidance[94]. This is what your policy papers and memos should focus on.

4.4.1.2 Alternative draft laws

Actually, most people are not opposed to someone else doing their work. If you only deliver technical analyses, graphs and lengthy legal opinions on certain draft law provisions asking the official to take them into consideration, you create a lot of work for the official drafting the law. But if you deliver your arguments, explain the problem you see in a certain provision and also come up with a written proposal for the official on how you think the draft law could be changed in the paragraph under discussion, all at the same time, you act constructively and take the work load off of him.

[94] Bouwen, Corporate Lobbying in the European Union, p. 5

Even though you cannot expect of course that your draft will find its way into the legislative process one-to-one, at least it enhances your chances of having your ideas being considered.

Tip

Deliver your own constructive proposals to the decision makers. On the basis of the EU institutions' draft law, provide for alternative legal provisions, slightly changing the relevant paragraphs only, but solving your problem. That makes it easier for the decision makers to follow you. No one wants to redraft the whole law.

Example 1

With its first so-called tobacco advertising directive the Commission wanted to forbid all possible ways of advertising for tobacco products. Understandably, the Commission wanted to avoid any circumvention of that intention by the tobacco and advertising industry. Knowing industry's creativity when it comes to undermining the law, the Commission used the comprehensive legal term of all "direct and indirect" advertising that should fall under the directive. In principle, that was a good idea to achieve this goal. But in its last consequence this provision lead to the fact that, for example, the Davidoff perfume and the Camel boots would have had to be taken off the market, since they were - very indirectly - advertising the respective tobacco products. But if - like in this case - the intention of the Commission was to limit European tobacco consumption, why ban a perfume and a pair of shoes from the market while the target itself, the cigarette, stays untouched?

A small legal provision with a huge, unintended impact. Explaining that problem, showing the consequences and offering an alternative legal provision replacing the word "indirect" in the directive can be a solution in such cases.

Though not compulsory, being a lawyer is a big advantage here. First, you don't just deliver someone else's legal draft, not being able to comment on it and do possible changes on the spot if necessary. Second, you are on a level playing field with the legislator, which makes it easier to talk.

Example 2

The EU drivers' license directive had the intention of lowering the risk of accidents amongst car drivers by lowering the tonnage of cars they are allowed to drive. Unfortunately, the tonnage was calculated – more or less arbitrarily – in a way that only truck drivers would have been allowed to drive caravans in the future.

Now, how is that family going to be able to rent a holiday caravan under those circumstances? Again, unintended impact with the need for an alternative legal provision.

If you are not a lawyer, then at least get one to accompany you in the process closely.

4.4.2 Meetings

As discussed, face-to-face meetings are the most important way that a decision maker can receive information. Usually, these meetings will take place on the basis of a written position paper you made so everyone knows what the discussion is about. Use these meetings to transport the main messages you laid down in your written statements. Be prepared, not only to stand up for your own arguments but also for the possible contradictory arguments people you meet might raise.

Know what you talk about. Since you are definitely not the only stakeholder the decision maker is listening to, there is no point in lying or hiding the truth. You will only ruin your reputation and the one of the stakeholder you lobby for. Your job is to deliver correct information and to explain why the position you have based on this data seems convincing to you. That means that, even though you deliver information, it is of course not enough to only have cold facts and objective truths. Most industries and interest groups have ample amounts of both of these. You need to turn these facts into arguments.

EU politics is built on compromise. Therefore, be aware that your position is one of many and will surely not be the only one taken into consideration in the legislative process. Always have a fallback position for a compromise in such meetings. No one will believe it if you say there are no alternatives – be it technically, politically or socially – to what you suggest.

Do not be too demanding or even make threats. The legendary meeting between Jack Welch and Competition Commissioner Mario Monti regarding the intended GE/Honeywell merger, at which the GE boss virtually kicked in the door, which he rather should have knocked on, is a perfect example of how not to do it. No Commission official depends on you and no MEP needs you or your money for his next election campaign. "Gunboat" methods therefore do not fly nearly so well in Brussels as in, for example, Washington.

4.4.3 Wining and dining

Wining and dining, creating friendly bonds and building relationships do no harm. There are therefore numerous events and venues in Brussels where you have the opportunity to rub shoulders with the

Tip

When meeting with a Commission official, an MEP, etc.

know the facts and possible counterarguments

know his background and biography

know his political network, friends and enemies

This kind of information is meanwhile accessible easily through commercial political databases such as www.europeanprofile.eu

major players whether it is at lectures, press conferences, receptions or other gala events. So get on the invitation lists by letting the others know that you are there.

Have a reception party yourself inviting other stakeholders and players. Be part of the community. Receptions can be important ways to raise general awareness of an issue and to stay in touch. If you have information for decision makers about issues which do not justify a meeting or which do not directly involve your stakeholder, place them here. As discussed, most decision makers are happy to receive information about up-coming issues. If you can deliver such information altruistically without even wanting something - even the better. That is probably the best way to stay in touch at all.

Tip

Which event is worth going to? How do you get an invitation? This kind of information is, meanwhile, accessible easily through event calendars in commercial databases such as www.europeanagenda.eu

Lunch meetings are best held in one of the many restaurants around either Place Luxembourg behind the Parliament or Place Jourdan, half way walking distance between the Commission, the Council and the Parliament.

However, receptions are poor ways to communicate a specific message or detail. It is important to differentiate between the formal meetings and the social environment in which you meet with decision makers and other stakeholders: There are on the one hand the meetings you have with the decision makers, usually in their offices. This is clear working environment. A lunch event with a Commission official or an MEP can have the character of a working meeting and therefore be the basis for exchanging thoughts on certain policy issues. But no decision maker wants to be bothered with the problem details you have regarding a certain draft law on energy regulation at 8 p.m. in the evening while trying to listen to the sounds of a classical string quartet after a hard working day.

The following events and receptions are a "must"
- Receptions of the regional representations, e.g. the "Oktoberfest" of the Representation of Bavaria. Everyone – including all politicians and officials – who wants to be part of the Brussels scene is to be found there.
- Receptions of company representations and associations, like the summer parties of the car producer BMW and Deutsche Post World Net ("Worldpost reception") or the annual reception of the banking associations. Generally good level and standard, usually some high-ranking politicians and officials.

But evening receptions do not exclude you from raising policy issues in a general way during a social conversation. EU policies sometimes even create a common basis for starting small talk since everyone at the events you attend is in effect more or less involved in them. But the surrounding is not the right one for a detailed discussion about it. Receptions usually take place between Tuesday and Thursday, because this is when the MEPs are back from their home constituencies and have not left for them again already. Furthermore, events are mostly limited to the weeks when the Parliament is in Brussels and not in Strasbourg. Therefore, there are few time slots for a mass of stakeholders trying to get the attention. This results in event-hopping most of the time, giving the decision makers, which try to cover at least some of the get-togethers, only about 1 hour for each event. During that time, the decision makers want to meet as many people as possible for a chat. So they will not be very happy to be blocked from that by your lament. If you do have a problem, address it that evening and arrange for a work meeting to do the follow up and the details.

Do not just join events. Arrange them yourself and thereby make use of events and receptions as a lobbying tool

- If you have an issue at stake, arrange a "lunch discussion" or "workshop" and invite the relevant stakeholders and decision makers.
- Alternatively, have a "theme event" to which you invite people in the evening. Rather arrange for a "walking dinner" than for a seated formal dinner so people can mix. Unlike in most EU capitals, there are few event agencies in Brussels since the event locations usually also provide for the catering.
- Have an interesting key note speaker, perhaps even from outside the usual Brussels arena and provide for information material from your perspective.
- Keep the speeches short. No one wants to listen to a 1 hour speech. That is not what people came for. Provide for unobtrusive escape routes and exits. No one should have the feeling to be bound to his seat when rather wanting to leave.

4.4.4 Media

A good lobbyist appreciates properly the role of the media: he not only knows how to explain, communicate and prepare a clear and concise argument to defend his point of view. He also does not neglect his relationship with the media, an indispensable forum for publicity and promotion. It is certainly not a good idea to be on the media's bad side. The media is an ubiquitous actor in politics. Often the framing of an issue, particularly for the public, is assisted by media portrayal. And since the EU's power structure is based on politics, it is not immune to this.

Imagine your mid-size stakeholder has a problem with some pharmaceutical giant blocking the market with some blockbuster patents. Don't you think it might be helpful for your abuse-of-a-dominant-position-complaint with the Commission if some leading newspapers and TV stations broadcasted about a potential danger for the European health systems due to the undue behaviour of that giant in this David versus Goliath constellation? It is not seldom that in those cases the issue is not even settled by the Commission but by the companies themselves. And not on grounds of competition law but for PR reasons. It has proved in the past that the potentially bad reputation the companies fear and the expected cost of rebuilding that reputation affects the companies' mind set and their position on policy issues enormously. Further, the immediate impact such negative media headlines have on the companies' stock listings, followed by poor analysts' credit ratings and therefore higher interest rates the companies have to pay on loans, puts the companies in difficult financial constraints and often gives reason enough for most companies to settle the issue – regardless of the legal situation. Public opinion is powerful. And having it on your side is not a bad thing.

This is to demonstrate the importance that the media can have in some battles. Importance that you must not underestimate. This is also to say that the lobbyist must have, among his various skills, an ability to communicate with the media. Certainly, exercising influence is not merely public relations. But one cannot deny them their proper place.

As for skills, you need the savoir-faire necessary to avoid the errors of a debutant. You do not improvise the night before a press conference. You do not meet a journalist and tell him what you would like to see him write. This professionalism in procedure is necessary in order to properly present the information. According to the form adopted, the message will pass perfectly - or less well. You want a quote, either in the newspaper or on TV? Put your problem in one sentence only. Not possible? Make it three, but short ones: always have in mind the cutter preparing the tape for the evening news. Give him a sentence he can use.

Make use of the media for your lobbying purposes. Living in a world dominated by mass media this is a useful instrument. A few rules of thumb:

- Treat journalists as partners. They are no enemies. Neither are they your friends.
- Journalists do not know everything. This is why they ask questions.
- Journalists want something to print or broadcast. This is why they need newsworthy and background information.
- Be honest and open hearted since journalists are looking for the truth.
- Do not try to "buy" them.

In any case, it is the same with media contacts as it is with officials.
You must build relationships with them that are carefully cultivated,
in order that they become more confidential. The world of accredited
journalists to the EU is not so large. You can create a network of correspondents from their ranks.

Which sources do those in power consult for information? Again,
different EU decision makers have different perceptions of which
source they trust most[95] (see chart on the next page).

Among printed media sources, the Financial Times is rated as
the best source of information on industry for the Commission and
Council, while MEPs opt first for their own national newspapers.
However, the MEPs rank the Financial Times quite highly as well.
The Council members also appear much more interested in their re-
spective national newspapers.

Since media has developed to a real power in most democracies, add-
ing to the legislative, executive and judiciary bodies, politicians and officials cannot ignore it. If the independent press is on your side, you will
have good arguments for your position being reflected in the drafts.

4.5 Grassroots

Remember the old elephant joke? "Where does a ten-ton elephant
sleep?" "Anywhere it wants". Grassroots is about the power of sheer
mass[96]. Grassroots efforts have been much more common in the US,
asking citizens for example to write their congressional representative a protest note on a certain policy issue. Is a traffic light needed
at the intersection of Hope and Pray Streets? Should new sidewalks
be constructed alongside Hazard Boulevard? Are more street lights
needed on Ominous Avenue? Those are typical grassroots matters[97].

[95] Burson-Marsteller, The Definitive Guide to Lobbying the European Institutions, p. 17
[96] Staples, Roots to power, p. 14
[97] Staples, Roots to power, p. 80

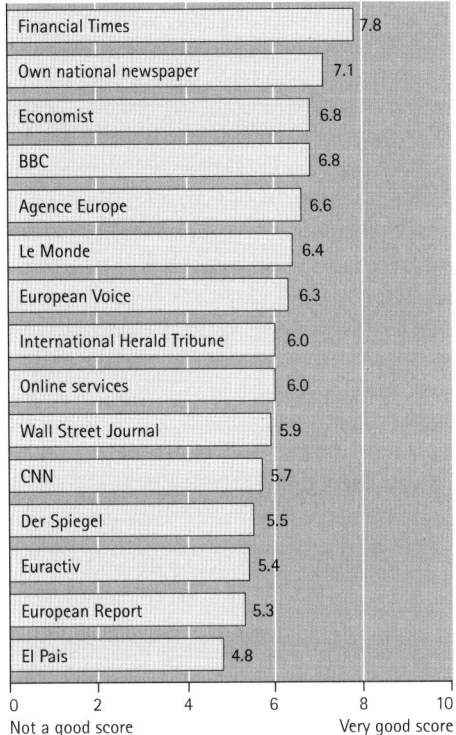

Key sources of information on industry

On a scale from 1–10, what are your key sources of information on industry

But even though grassroots have been classically used for community issues, they have developed to an own lobbying means by now, which you can make use of. By gathering many people doing the same, the intention is to put pressure on the representatives directly from their voters making them fear for their reelection. The supranational structure of the EU, different languages, and the absence of a common European people have made this style of lobbying, if not unfeasible in the EU, at least not worth the cost in the past. However, due to the Internet, Weblogs and other media tools, this lobbying practice has a potential in the EU, also, as it has been demonstrated lately again with regard to the REACH initiative on the chemicals policy of the EU.

Grassroots campaign of the European Public Health Alliance (EPHA) on the chemicals policy of the EU (REACH)[98]

How does grassroots lobbying work? Usually, even though grass-roots campaigns claim to be the voice of the people, to make this voice heard they need to be organised professionally. In the US this is mostly done by consultants, in the EU so far by the respective associations and by many NGOs[99].

[98] http://www.epha.org/a/209
[99] http://www.apcusa.com/grassroots.htm

Grassroots lobbying usually includes

- Emails and letters, being prepared on behalf of the people signing up for a certain policy issue. To collect unique and original letters instead of mass emails this is partly even done on a face-to-face basis by assisting the letter writer in putting their own thoughts on paper. The letters are then being mailed to elected and regulatory officials and to the local newspapers, to turn around public stances taken by opponents in political battles.
- Plebiscite petition signatures, which means gathering masses of signatures to demonstrate public support or opposition to an issue.
- Grassroots networks, which is about having extensive and experienced ground forces available whether the needs are for door-to-door activists, workers at local super markets, etc.
- Third party organisation development, meaning the building from scratch of special interest organisations, Websites, Blogs, fund raising programmes, etc. to add additional leverage to the policy subjects.
- Telephone calls, utilising affiliated telephone banks and call centers to contact selected people and informing them of the key issues during a campaign. If they are motivated to support the issue, they are being asked if they would like to talk directly to key members of the governing body making the decision. If the answer is yes, calls are patched directly to the decision maker's office.

Grassroots mobilisation can be a very effective tool for matters that you, as a lobbyist, think might be best solved politically and emotionally, for example, due to the lack of solid arguments. In those cases it especially makes sense to put pressure on the EU institutions by involving the masses, the voters. No government or institution in a democracy is able to neglect the free will of the people. So make use of it.

V. Lobbying experiences

What are the experiences of those involved in day-to-day EU lobbying? How do decision makers feel about Lobbyists? What do they regard as useful? When do they start to feel uncomfortable? How should Lobbyists behave in their eyes? Representatives of all three EU institutions laid down their thoughts on this, to help you understand how to lobby best. After that, Brussels representatives from companies, associations, NGO, national governments and consultancies share their experiences of EU lobbying with you – to help you do a better job. Take their advise.

1. The European Commission

1.1 Siim Kallas, Vice President of the European Commission in charge of Administration, Audit and Anti-fraud

Lobbying for Transparency

The European public is entitled to expect efficient, accountable and service minded public institutions. The European Commission believes that compliance with the highest standards of transparency is a condition for the legitimacy of a modern administration. In today's information society, transparency is our means to communicate that we act with integrity and credibility. The Commission has set itself high standards: All Commissioners are bound by a Code of Conduct[100] which provides for ethical guidelines on their activities and asks for a declaration of their financial interests to show and ensure their integrity. Already in 2002, the Commission also adopted minimum standards for consultation[101] to create a transparent and coherent general framework for consultations of interested parties. To further pursue these objectives, the European Commission launched the European Transparency Initiative in November 2005[102], followed by a Green Paper on the European Transparency Initiative adopted in May 2006[103]. The main goal is to increase openness and accessibility of EU institutions, and make the Union's institutions more accountable to the public. To do this, the Commission is proposing that informa-

[100] SEC(2004) 1487/2; [101] COM(2002) 704; [102] SEC(2005) 1300; [103] COM(2006) 194

tion on all beneficiaries of EU funds should be disclosed. This will increase accountability on the use of the EU taxpayer's money, and would facilitate a well-informed public debate on the benefits of action at the EU level. Another important measure proposed is to make lobbying at the EU level more transparent. Since this is a handbook for lobbyists, I will concentrate on this aspect of the European Transparency Initiative.

"Where's the problem?"

Fortunately, we have had no Abramoff-type scandal in Brussels. But we must not sit back and simply trust that it couldn't happen. Being the centre for the institutions of the European Union, Brussels has – next to Washington D.C. – over the years become one of two main hubs for lobbying activities worldwide. Around 15,000 lobbyists work in the Belgian capital to represent the interests of many different groups before the EU. And there is reason to believe that the lobbying industry in Brussels might continue growing as American companies discover the importance of Brussels as a place of global policymaking. The growing market that lobbyists see in Brussels reflects the positive attitude the Commission has always had towards consultation and interest representation[104]. Lobbying is an important and legitimate part of EU policy decision-making processes, regardless of whether it is carried out by individual citizens or companies, civil society organisations and other interest groups or firms working on behalf of third parties. Each decision-making process needs proper information from different angles, and the European Commission is committed to broad consultations before exercising its right of initiative to propose new EU law. However, at times, concerns are voiced about lobbying practices going beyond the legitimate representation of interests. Without any doubt, fraudulent and corruptive practices cannot be tolerated. Neither does distorted information given to the EU institutions about the possible economic, social or environmental impact of a draft legislative proposal serve the legitimate aim. Moreover, questions are raised whether it is legitimate for the EU to financially support groups, which then represent particular interests before the policy makers. These concerns question not only the credibility of EU policy-making, but also the integrity of lobbyists, and the European Commission takes them seriously.

When the Abramoff case occurred in the US, the Commission asked itself whether it could have happened in Brussels as well. Of course, there are obvious differences between Brussels and Wash-

[104] see the first official document in this regard: Communication "An Open and Structured Dialogue Between the Commission and Special Interest Groups", SEC(1992) 2272 final.

ington such as the number of people involved in lobbying and the amounts spent on it (in Washington, 25,500 lobbyists are currently billing $ 2.1 billion a year, while in Brussels, one estimate sets the total annual of all lobbying budgets at 90 million). The style in which lobbying is undertaken is largely shaped by the political system and the institutional structure to which the activity is targeted. Here, the electoral campaigns give a very different connecting factor for lobbyists: candidates for Congress in the US must seek corporate political support and money and consider corporations, NGOs and other associations as their electorate. Another distinction is that alternation between public functions and business or interest groups and vice versa is less frequent in Brussels than in Washington.

Yet, it would be utterly naïve not to see that the American and the European systems also have many things in common. Brussels and Washington are widely recognised as the two main lobbying capitals of the world. Decisions and legislation in both places affect the lives and interests of hundreds of millions of citizens. Furthermore, even though Washington and Brussels are on different continents, their lobbying communities are not on different planets. Some of the companies are the same, and a lot of cross-fertilisation – positive and negative – takes place. Moreover, in both places there are human beings involved. It would be arrogant, and indeed a sign of ignorance, to claim that European politicians and high-ranking officials cannot be corrupted.

The Commission feels that the demand for integrity should not be limited to public institutions. Organisations, groups and persons in the ambit of European institutions which offer advice, represent clients, provide data or defend public causes do participate in EU policy-making and should therefore also be accountable. Lobbyists can have considerable influence on legislation, in particular on proposals of a technical nature. But their transparency is too deficient in comparison to the impact of their activities. Citizens should be able to know who they are, what they do and what they stand for. The same applies for Non Governmental Organisations. Many NGO's rely on public funding, some from the Commission. For those, the word 'non' is rather fictitious. Some of the NGO's receiving funds from the Commission describe on their website one of their main tasks as: 'lobbying the Commission'. The 'European Transparency Initiative' seeks to increase transparency also in these networks.

Four concrete measures proposed

In its Transparency Initiative, the European Commission proposes four concrete measures to create greater transparency in the relations between the Commission and interest representatives:

(1) A Code of conduct for lobbyists

In Europe, the traditional concept puts the onus on the ethical behaviour of the institutions themselves, and we must not fall short in this regard. However, the Commission feels that they should be countered by integrity rules for lobbyists. Thus, we ask the lobbying profession to establish a code of conduct. Already in the Communication on special interest groups in 1992, lobbyists were invited to adopt their own codes of conduct. At that time, the Commission proposed 3 main ingredients: a commitment to act in an honest manner and to declare the interest a lobbyist represents, not to disseminate misleading information and not to offer any form of inducement in order to obtain information or receive preferential treatment. As a result of this, various umbrella organisations of consultants and consultancy firms have adopted voluntary codes of conduct. I clearly see this as a development in the right direction. However, in the Green Paper the Commission calls for a comprehensive approach: so far, only consultants adhere to the established codes. Neither lobbyists who are permanent employees of interest groups nor other groups of interest representatives who occasionally engage in lobbying activities (e.g. law firms and think tanks) fall within their scope. Furthermore, the current system relies on self-discipline while the Commission feels that an effective enforcement system is indispensable for its credibility. Thus, it appears necessary to consolidate the existing codes and put in place a common enforcement and sanction system trusted by all. The Commission deems it important that the lobbying profession takes ownership of the standards for its work. In the Green Paper we suggest that the lobbying society of Brussels itself develops a common code of conduct, applicable to all lobbyists, monitored by a special umbrella organisation.

(2) Voluntary registration of lobbyists

A common code of conduct would enhance the credibility of the lobbying profession. To provide for public accountability, the Commission proposes to develop and manage a web-based voluntary registration system for all interest groups and lobbyists. So far, there is no mandatory regulation on reporting or registering lobby activities. Registers provided by lobbyists' organisations in the EU are voluntary, incomprehensive and do not provide much information on the specific interests represented or how it is financed. To qualify for entry in the proposed register, applicants would be asked to provide information on whom they represent, what their mission is and how they are funded. Also, they would have to subscribe to the common code of conduct mentioned above. In return, groups and lobbyists who register would have the opportunity to indicate their specific interests and, in return, would be alerted to consultations in those specific areas. Consequently, only lobbyists who have registered would be automatically alerted by the Commission. For the general public, the register would give access to information about groups engaged in lobbying the Commission.

(3) Minimal standards for consultation

The information provided for in the registration system would, in connection with the Commission's minimal standards for consultation, allow public scrutiny of the lobbyist's input in EU policy-making. The minimal standards for consultation oblige the Commission, amongst others, to publish participants' contributions to public consultations on the internet. Linking these to the background of the participants in the register enables every citizen to comprehend the consultation processes. The minimum standards apply to consultations on the Commission's major policy proposals as well as to consultations on Green Papers. Moreover, Commission departments are encouraged to apply these standards to other consultation exercises as well. The minimum standards have been in force since the beginning of 2003. By the end of 2005, the Commission had completed more than one hundred major proposals and 26 Green Papers to which they applied. With the Green Paper European Transparency Initiative, the Commission now seeks stakeholders' views on this framework for activities of interest representatives and the need for new initiatives.

(4) Common ethical standards

All 3 EU institutions are involved in policy-making processes. Thus, the Commission considers it necessary to ensure an "ethical level playing field" between all institutions. Only if that is provided for can the institutions be a consistent counterpart for EU lobbyists and role-model a coherent level of ethical standards towards the public. To that end, the Commission has relaunched the idea of an inter-institutional Advisory Group on ethics in public life as already proposed by the Commission in 2000.

Conclusion

The Transparency Initiative will enhance the legitimacy of EU deci-sion-making through a number of concrete initiatives, including in the area of lobbying.

The European Commission encourages the Brussels lobby society to self-regulate. Having heard the reaction for the lobby profession, I am confident that there is support for this approach and, indeed, the proposed measures hold a number of benefits for the lobbying community itself.

For one, transparency enhances the credibility of the profession. Looking at the impact of the Abramoff scandal in the US, we must take preventive steps. A poll from the Gallup Institute in May showed that, while in January 38% of Americans believed most members of Congress to be corrupt, after Abramoff that figure rose to 47%. One might imagine what people think of the lobbyists then.

Secondly, transparency enhances the credibility of individual lobbyists. Through voluntary registration, lobbyists demonstrate that they are willing to argue their case publicly, showing that they believe their facts to be reliable and accurate.

Thirdly, transparent lobbying is more effective lobbying. It may reach a wider audience, and it is likely to get more focused atten-tion. Certainly, a politician is more inclined to listen to the advice of someone whose interests are clear than of someone who does not disclose.

For all these reasons, I believe that it is both timely and possible to take concrete steps to enhance the transparency of lobbying the EU institutions.

1.2 Alexander Schaub, former Director General Internal Market and Services of the European Commission

Lobbying – Experiences and Expectations

Looking back to many years in the European Commission, I can underline the fact that the Brussels scene is a real "El Dorado" for all types of lobbyism. Where legislative proposals are drafted, where political decisions are made, where the decision makers are "at hand", there is some margin for manoeuvre for influence from consultants, law firms or individual companies. With the further integration of the European Union and the increasing powers of the European in-stitutions, lobbying also developed quite significantly.

The way lobbying has evolved can also be seen from comparing architecture in Brussels. If it were true that lobbying still took place in the anterooms of the assembly, the European Parliament's imposing halls and salons would suggest that all of Europe's lobbying happens there. The rather modest entry to the numerous European Commission buildings would suggest that these must be quite uninteresting places for lobbyists. But drawing such conclusions just from architecture would be wrong - no experienced lobbyist would ignore the Commission just because of the size of their entry halls. It is a matter of fact: making your voice heard in the European Union's "corridors of power" is vital, when legislation that could have a profound impact upon your business or industry is being discussed. This concerns not only the legislative bodies in the EU - Council and Parliament - but also the European Commission which has the monopoly of initiative and is preparing the formal proposals for further treatment by the legislators. The Commission issues communications and recommendations as well, which do not provide legislative draft rules but give guidance on certain issues. It is obvious: the earlier lobbying starts to work on the ground and the broader it is targeted, the higher are the chances of successful influence. The Commission, therefore, is an important target for articulation of interests.

Having served as an official of the European Commission for a long time, I would like to share some reflections about networking and lobbying gained from this experience. During these years I covered many policy areas, most of them at the heart of business interests. And I have witnessed the whole range of the "art" of lobbying – from blunt and aggressive "attacks" of the "kamikaze"-type activists to reliable, long-standing relations based on provision of technical, verifiable information. No need to elaborate that the first type is not really a sustainable approach.

1.2.1 Networks

No doubt: Networks are essential for a constructive and efficient lobbying effort. A huge bureaucratic organisation, like the European Commission, is in this respect of particular interest. One of the most obvious networks within the European Commission is the officials coming from the same Member State. But it is often striking – and in a way reassuring – how informal and little-organised these groups are, not only regarding the big Member States with a huge number of officials, but also regarding smaller Member States. The Commission itself does not have structures in place to get people from a given Member State together. This is sometimes done from the outside. The Permanent Representations or the offices of the Regions can and do play an important role in this.

As most large organisations, the European Commission has many other networks that function in parallel with the official hierarchical structure. There are for example the current or former members of the cabinets of the Commissioners who form a distinctly multinational network group. The experience of years of cabinet life creates a kind of "comradeship" which lasts long and might still show results much later, when the officials return to work in a particular Directorate General. I rely here on my personal experience: after many years in different cabinets, I joined "the services" and met quite a few old cabinet colleagues in different functions throughout the Brussels scene. Lesser known networks within the European Commission are those of people sharing the same academic experience. The College of Europe in Brugge is just one example, with a large number of former students working in the European Commission, but also in the Parliament, Council and many other institutions.

More often one may find specialised lobbyists and consultants, law firms, or even individual companies being very efficient in the use of networks. However, this does not mean that these players always get it right. I remember an occasion where a big company tried to use the network of German officials working in the European Commission. All the high ranks of the company were present at a reception organised in one of the particular places of the European quarter. But the nice environment did not balance the mistakes being made. First, there was a presentation lasting more than one hour. Power-Point might be an asset, but after the fortieth slide one will inevitably get bored. A lengthy panel discussion followed by a ping-pong of self-congratulatory comments. No plans for the future, no vision. Instead of presenting something new and attractive it looked pretty much like the celebration of the anniversary of a communist statesman. In the meantime, it had become almost nine in the evening. No food had been served. The participants, already bored, started to get annoyed, or hungry, or both. They began to leave. Quite clear that the company did not get its message across on this occasion.

1.2.2 Lobbying the Commission
No one has more contacts with the Commission than governments and the public administration of Member States. One would therefore think that they have acquired a lot of networking and lobbying expertise. Some Member States are indeed very effective in presenting

a clear position at all levels of negotiation and representation. However, this is not always the case. Some administrations often struggle to even have a position at all. One often-used way of weakening the position of a Member State in discussions with the Commission is to present contradicting positions. A letter from a regional minister who feels the matter is not being treated well at home and tries to circumvent his own government may oppose a point made by the central government. Alternatively, ministers of the same government may sometimes follow inconsistent strategies in their contacts with the Commission. In some instances, contacts with representatives from the Member States are verging on comedy. How would you feel as a Director General to come to a meeting arranged as confidential, and be greeted by the press brought along by the representative from the Member State? Of course, these examples concern individual lobby groups or companies as well. Another point to mention is a new aggressive style of lobbying the Commission is exposed to. During the discussions on the Computer Implemented Inventions Directive, technically well-equipped lobby groups sent thousands of e-mails per day, organised demonstrations to block the entrance etc. The Commission appreciates useful information and arguments but there should be a limit to this kind of approach, which risks being counter-productive.

One could add quite a few of similar stories, but I better turn to some positive "techniques" of lobby work with the European Commission, as it is surprising how often lobbyists do not respect even basic rules:

- When calling, indicate what company you work for, and explain who your client is.
- When asking for appointments, clearly identify the topics to be discussed.
- Contact the responsible unit in the first place - experts dealing with a file do not appreciate if a lobbyist circumvents them by trying to get a commitment from the Member of the Commission without ever having contacted them.
- Sending letters or emails to dozens of people in the European Commission risks causing more coordination work than enthusiasm for the ideas.

There are many ways to lobby. One can block roads or flood e-mail accounts, demonstrate in front of the Commission's Berlaymont building or boycott supermarkets. A CEO may call saying that there are thousands of jobs at stake or a minister indicating a vote of confidence looming in the national Parliament unless the Commission does this or that. Looking back over the years, I think that none of these practices or tactics is really effective. They only indicate that there is a problem and that the ones responsible are not able to deal properly with it. However, they do not offer solutions. If there is a real issue with a European Commission proposal, or if a problem requires action, I found it much more effective to receive a clear and fair description of that problem, with suggestions how it could be solved. It is the argument that matters. And I can assure the reader that, as a general rule, the Commission will well weigh up the arguments, check and re-check, evaluate and examine, before it will adopt a proposal.

1.2.3 Evolutions in the Commission over the past years

Over the years, the nature of lobbying the European Commission changed quite a lot. Ten years ago, a key function of lobbyists was simply to search documents for their clients. It was important to know whom to ask to get a copy. Today, most is on the internet. The rules about access to documents have changed dramatically. Most documents of the European institutions are now available to every citizen. No reason has to be given for asking, but reasons have to be given by the Commission if access is denied. Another important change in the European Commission has been the increased focus on "civil society" and "good governance". The aim is to promote a culture of dialogue and participation. One could describe this as introducing a more organised, systematic and transparent way of listening to lobby groups. Before the Commission embarks on a new policy initiative, a broad and open consultation process is launched. One does not need to be a well-connected lobbyist anymore to get to know about such an initiative.

Over recent years, there are many examples for this change in approach. For the past few years in the Directorate General for the Internal Market we launched many of these consultations asking for input from all sides of the stakeholders. This approach is well received. Just to give one example: in reply to the consultation on the future of European patent policy, the Commission received more than 2000 contributions. What I find particularly interesting about this process is that not only does the Commission invite for comments, it also publishes these comments. Thus, they become transparent for everyone. However, this effort to listen more, and to listen to as many as possible, has a serious impact on the staff resources of the European Commission. Preparation, coordination and evaluation of these consultations require enormous work. Therefore, one result might be that the time allocated to each voice is becoming shorter, because it has to be shared with others. Furthermore   and this is an important aspect of the work of the Commission – there must be a "reserved area". Transparency is good, but there is a necessity to keep a space for reflection that allows the Commission to discuss options properly in the preparatory stages of legislation. Also, the Commission should be reasonable: a closed system will produce bad policies because it is deaf and disconnected, but an open system without a period of internal reflection will turn decision making institutions into talk shows.

A second interesting aspect of the changing nature of lobbying is what I call the "two-way" lobbying process: the European Commission is a target for lobbying by others, but it also has to ensure its own lobbying vis-à-vis others. It took a while, but over the past years, the European Commission has learned a lot about the need to also do its own lobbying. And it was a hard way to go, learning some unpleasant lessons. The famous Services Directive is just one example that a strategic approach from the side of the Commission including communicating the proposal and lobbying would have helped to have more fact-based discussions than emotional ones. Members of the Commission and the officials doing the daily work must become even more professional about explaining their actions and policies to the outside world. Good communication is more than ever needed. And results are visible: Many Directorates General are becoming familiar in professionally working with the European Parliament or with non governmental organisations to sell Commission policy.

1.2.4 Outlook
But where is the train heading to? What could be future aspects of lobbying the European Commission? I strongly believe that in order to remain successful, lobbying will have to adapt and change for several reasons. First, the Commission has recently started an ambitious exercise in staff mobility. The effects of this are only emerging slowly, but I believe this will have a strong impact on lobbying work. The days of Director Generals, Directors or Heads of Unit dealing with the same special field for fifteen or more years are over. Every couple of years, a new face will appear. The same will apply to most desk officers. I always supported this policy. It not only keeps the officials flexible and open for new fields of work, but it also avoids having to

wear blinkers and listen to the same type of arguments all the time. The wind of change is good for the administration, too. The lobbyist will therefore continuously have to deal with new correspondents. New faces appear, new styles apply. Since the different levels of hierarchy will not change jobs at the same time, one will more often see that at least every second year, either the Director General, the Director, or the Head of Unit will be new. This increased mobility within the Commission will have other consequences as well. There will be new and changing networks. The Commission's work will also have to become more rule-based and better documented. Rules and procedures will have to become simpler to allow for regular mobility of staff.

A second important change concerns the dynamics of negotiations at the level of the Members of the Commission and at the level of their cabinets. With the enlarged EU of 25 or 27, the landscape is becoming more fragmented. Although the issues are similar, they will be with no doubt more complex than before. The number of lobbyists and stakeholders established permanently in Brussels has increased significantly. Since 2004, the five big Member States are only represented by a single Commissioner, instead of two. Until enlargement, a concerted effort by the Commissioners from two of the big Member States meant that four out of twenty members of the College took a common position. This was sometimes quite effective. Now, the same effort by the Commissioners nominated by these Member States will mobilise just two persons out of twenty-five. The effect of this mathematics will also apply at the cabinet level, where much of the preparatory work for the weekly meeting of the Commission is done. Discussions there have already become more difficult to predict because of the increased number. Today, the discussions between the various Directorates General of the European Commission about a draft proposal can be quite intense and may lead to substantial changes to a text proposed by one Directorate General. It can be quite effective to lobby a Directorate General other than the one drafting the original proposal, but involved in these internal debates. As a consequence of all this, I would expect that the position of the Commissioner proposing a text may become even stronger than it is today. For lobbyists, this will mean that they will have to pay even more attention to the work at the level of the Directorates General, and to the member of the Commission responsible for a given topic. However, time is becoming increasingly scarce for the top people in the Commission. This is another result of enlargement.

The third point to be mentioned: Commission staff will not increase much because of enlargement. Commission teams dealing with 15 Member States in the past now have to share their time amongst 25 without much additional resources. This will mean that in particular the Members of the Commission and top management staff may become less available in the future for simple numerical reasons. For lobbyists, this may well mean they should focus more on lower level staff in order to get their message across.

A fourth element is the new European Transparency Initiative (ETI) announced by Commissioner Kallas (see Kallas above). The ETI, as outlined in the Green Paper published 3 May 2006, aims to strengthen the openness and accessibility of the European Commission and to make the EU generally more accountable to the public. It is, among other things, intended to correct the current lack of transparency around the estimated 15,000 lobbyists working to influence the EU institutions. This might include codes of conduct for lobbyists, common principles and a voluntary register. The credibility of such a system will, however, depend on its proper monitoring, rules of enforcement and high participation rate of lobbyists. This time the lobbyists should contribute their own views on their work. We will see what consequences will arise from that exercise.

2. The European Parliament

Charles Henry Plumb, former President of the European Parliament and Member of the House of Lords, Westminster

Lobbying has always been part and parcel of policy-making and legislating, and always will be. While in some cultures it has taken longer for this process to be viewed as mainstream activity, there is nothing more natural than particular groups wanting to make known their concerns to those who have the power to do something about it. Within my career, I moved from lobbying on behalf of the National Farmers' Union to being on the receiving end as an MEP.

During my twenty years as a member of the European Parliament, there was never a time that I did not receive representations from interest groups or individuals. This took place just as much when I was a rank and file MEP as when I was Leader of a Group, President of the Agriculture Committee or indeed President of Parliament. On one occasion, I received over 1000 letters from people approving the culling of baby seals!

The lobbying began at Birmingham Airport. Waiting to board my flight to Brussels, I was constantly approached by deputations on their way for some meeting at EU headquarters. From the time that I entered the first directly elected European Parliament in 1979 up to the time I stepped down from my last official post in that institution in 2006, there was a constant and steady growth in the lobby business. This growth became a veritable explosion after the Maastricht Treaty gave co-decision power to the European Parliament.

As a hunting man, I work on the principle that you shoot where the ducks are. The fact that Brussels is teeming with lobbyists of all shapes and sizes, from environmentalists to industrialists, from farming organisations to consumer groups; this fact is testament to the very significant power of the European Parliament in making decisions that have a real impact on the lives of hundreds of millions of Europeans.

Of course, not all lobbyists are equally effective. Boris Johnson described the art of being a good lobbyist as getting up early, reading the „Pink Paper" from cover to cover, phoning all your clients with the news gleaned from the FT before they get to their desks at 9am. You can then go back to bed, having earned your money for the day.

3. The Council of the European Union

Gerard Collins, former President of the Council of the European Union and Irish Minister for Foreign Affairs

In terms of the Council of Ministers, in the past, lobbying consisted primarily of contacts made in the national capital, whether to the Minister, officials in the Ministry or indeed via the standing committees in the National Parliaments. I saw my role in the Presidency of the EU as something of a sherpa, trying to steer the decision making process to a conclusion. The scope for influencing the overall agenda of the Presidency is limited. The usual way things are done is for the incoming Presidency to agree the programme with the President of the European Commission.

There are always a number of main items that are going to feature because they are at that point in the procedure. As President in Office, my main aim in setting the agenda was to make sure that there was consensus on same items from the Member States. Of course, differences later arise when it comes to the time for final decision making. But it would have been inappropriate for me to be listening to particular lobbies at the early planning stage and it just didn't happen.

Clearly, far more lobbying takes place within the Commission and the Parliament and there are occasions when lobbyists have developed such a network of contacts within the system, that they are informed about events before some of the legislators. Nevertheless, lobbies are certainly needed and they have a role in putting across their case for consideration. They must make their own position clear to the legislators and ensure, as far as they can, that it is given due consideration, properly analysed and evaluated. What is certain is that lobbyists have a right to be heard and should not be ignored.

EU legislation frequently deals with highly technical matters where the solutions may not be apparent. Legislators cannot possibly be experts in every field and therefore the activity of representative interest groups is helpful in the overall process.

My own experience has certainly been that lobbying has a key role to play in the legislative process and I would wish to see this role continue. Naturally, there need to be adequate safeguards in place at the same time to ensure that no individual is compromised. The proper functioning of the EU legislative process, including Council, Commission and Parliament, requires that lobbyists play their role. In order for this process to remain healthy and working in the public interest, the lobbying industry needs to be properly set within appropriate operational guidelines.

4. Companies

4.1 Hanns R. Glatz, Delegate of the Board of Management of DaimlerChrysler, External Affairs and Public Policy European Affairs, Brussels

EU Lobbying – some conclusions from my experience over the last 36 years

When I came to Brussels on 1 May 1970, much was different but lobbying was already known at that time. Admittedly, the number of "lobbyists" was much smaller, but the striking difference was, that only very few companies – and in fact also very few industry sectors – had realised at that time that it was important to be present in Brussels. The first "representative offices" were opened primarily by the large multinational companies of American parentage. They knew about lobbying from Washington and for them the European Commission was an important governmental authority which appreciated their economic weight much more than the individual national governments of those countries where they had sales companies or plants.

Business in general was represented through UNICE from the beginning of the process of European integration. Sector organisations came later – and most of them in the form of two-tier organisations, the so-called Liaison Committees (or better "comités de liaison" because at that time the lingua franca of the Community world was French). Since then, more and more European sector organisations have been created in Brussels with a clear trend towards direct company participation in so far as this is feasible. In parallel with the discussion about the division of responsibilities between the European Union and its Member States there is a process of readjustment of powers, budgets and relevance between the old national and the new European sector organisations.

The representation of interests at that time was, perhaps, simpler. Three examples:

The institutions were much smaller; it was easier to know personally most of the decision makers and opinion leaders in Brussels. The European Parliament had only a fraction of the powers it holds today. Many of the important decisions in the Council of Ministers had to be taken by unanimous vote. It was easy to hide behind one's own national government to block an unwelcome decision. It was, how-

ever, more difficult to promote any initiative that needed approval
by all 6, 9, 10 or 12 members before the widespread introduction of
majority voting in the Council through the "Single European Act",
which entered into force in 1987.

There was also a wider culture of "dialogue" between interested par
ties and the Commission. Today this is largely replaced by "consultation". Most likely this deplorable change is due to two developments:
the growing number of stakeholders due to the enlargements of the EU,
greater interest of stakeholders to participate in the political process at
EU level, and the emergence of the "civil society" – the desire of various
groups of people to represent their interests directly because of a growing lack of confidence in our representative democratic institutions.

And finally, important areas of EU policy were not as densely regulated as they are today. For example, the approval of state aid for
new investments, for many years, was an issue for discussion with
officials from DG IV (the numbering at the time for DG Competition); a legal framework for the competition aspects of distribution
and servicing agreements in the auto sector in the form of a block
exemption regulation was not adopted before 1985.

Strangely enough, however, not much has changed with regard
to the principles which render lobbying successful.

4.1.1 Representative – Lobbyist

A lobbyist is a person that knows perfectly well the decision making
processes and has access to key decision makers. She or he advises
on how to best present the arguments to whom, or even intervenes
on behalf of an interested party.

A good "EU representative" of a business firm, an association
or any other organisation, however, needs to know more and to do
more. She or he must be the interface between a given organisation
and the EU institutions, diplomats, journalists and other organisations. And profound knowledge of the own organisation's interests,
products, plans etc. is one of the biggest assets – because it opens
doors to opinion leaders and decision makers.

4.1.2 Networks

There is the saying "Make friends when you do not need them". And
repeatedly I have learned how important this advice is for EU representatives and lobbyists. Building up networks inside one's own
organisation is as important as building networks in Brussels. Very
often, important questions need to be answered promptly. Then it is

useful to know the expert or the competent person in your organisation that can help you. And when you wish to intervene in the EU
decision making process, it can be done much more easily and effectively if you talk to somebody who knows and trusts you.

4.1.3 Obtain the relevant information

The first scandal about bad behaviour of lobbyists was triggered by
a person that took with him so many of the working documents laid
out in a European Parliament's committee meeting room that there
was no longer a sufficient number of these documents available for
all MEPs. At the time, these documents were selling well at good
prices. This time is over. Nearly all EP working documents are available online. The same is true for many documents of the Commission.
There are daily news-bulletins available in hardcopy and online. To
read them, it is not necessary to be physically present in Brussels.

However, documents and news are only part of what a good representative needs to know and to report to her or his organisation.
To hear the grass grow, to put things into the right context, to assess
what is really relevant for your organisation, to translate from Brussels speak into an understandable language, to reduce an 80 page
Commission Communication to a one pager, you need to be part of
the Brussels community – and for many organisations it is worth
while setting up a representative office in Brussels to get all this.

4.1.4 Act in due time and at the right place

EU decision making processes are complicated and complex. A
graphic presentation of the steps necessary to adopt an internal market directive looks like a chemical plant. Of course, it is always best
to influence policy papers or legislative acts when the first draft is
conceived. However, even if you are successful, you can never be
sure of your victory until the policy paper or the legal act is finally
adopted. Hence you must know the processes and the junctions when
somebody else or you yourself have a chance to exercise influence.

The EU institutions are governed by a relatively straight division
of responsibilities. Once the Commission has adopted a proposal for
a directive, it will be largely in the hands of the European Parliament
and the Council working group to make or propose amendments.
In theory the Commission could intervene in any moment before a
proposal is finally adopted – but is it politically strong enough in
your particular case? Moreover, the best amendment is useless if
presented to an MEP five minutes after the deadline for the presenta-

tion of amendments – unless you know the rules about presenting oral amendments in the voting session and you can motivate MEPs accordingly.

4.1.5 Do not rely on personal, political, national, or linguistic relations alone

In national lobbying it is mostly important to be well integrated into the network of the governing party or a regional group to which top politicians belong. This is the result of the fact that practically everywhere in democratic Europe political majorities control the government (mostly including both executive and legislative powers). The EU does not know government majorities: The Commission is composed of (presently) 25 people of different nationalities, different languages, and different political leanings. The same is true for the Council of Ministers. And even in the European Parliament, the large blocks of the EPP or PES often divide up internally on specific questions. Yes, there are European political parties but they are not (yet) as uniform or disciplined as national parties (mostly) are.

And if you think you can get a better understanding with one of your compatriots (e.g. inside the Commission), you may quickly find out that there is none of them in any relevant position. Hence, build your networks primarily according to relevant positions, and take all the other elements: language, political affiliation, regional origin, as additional elements that might create a positive climate for your discussion.

4.1.6 Look for allies

Particularly individual companies suffer from the fact that their relative importance at EU level is less than that at national level. On the other hand, the huge number of organised interests is very confusing for European decision makers and makes it very difficult for them to identify exactly the relevant interests they need to take into consideration. Hence, the need of visibility, representativeness and clarity obliges lobbyists to concentrate their efforts and seek alliances.

Thus there is no contradiction in the co-existence of branch organisations at European level and EU representative offices of all their members – as it is the case in the automotive sector. The BARs (Brussels Automotive Representatives) work closely together with ACEA, agree on common positions and e.g. share the work of talking to the many MEPs involved in relevant legislative projects. It is much more convincing to present a position shared by all vehicle manufacturers – and perhaps also the pertinent trade union organisations – than to explain the position of a single company only.

4.1.7 Use simple, credible and convincing arguments

As said before, the EU decision making processes are complicated and involve people of different nationalities, political affiliation, culture, language, professional background, etc. On the other hand, many of the issues subject to EU policies or legislation are highly technical and complex. Hence, it is very tempting for the specialists to provide an absolutely correct but very complex line of argument why something needed to be regulated or done differently. The art of the lobbyist is to simplify (not falsify!) this line of argument to the extent that it can be understood by all decision makers involved and can be easily adopted by one or the other of them as her or his own opinion.

4.1.8 Be prepared for compromises

The EU follows a culture of compromise. Hardly any of the Commission's proposals have ever been sent back by the European Parliament or the Council of Ministers as superfluous, inappropriate or wrong (and there were such proposals). Hence, it is pretty hopeless to develop a lobby line geared at the total elimination of a proposal or of a specific provision in a proposal. The most promising way still is to anticipate the sort of compromise which might sell.

The difficulty in this process is to determine the moment and the circumstances when such a compromise should be proposed and by whom. Often it is most appropriate to leave it to a Member State or to an MEP to be the initiator. Also the Commission could do it in the process of giving its opinion on amendments proposed by either the EP or the Council. Compromises proposed by an interested party always create suspicion unless they are jointly proposed by parties with divergent interests.

4.1.9 Never cheat

Credibility with officials and politicians is the biggest asset of an EU representative. And while there are thousands of lobbyists in Brussels, Brussels is a village where news spread with the speed of light. It is quickly known if somebody tried to influence a decision making process with a lie, or identified herself or himself wrongly and this person or organisation will encounter big difficulties in being believed again.

4.1.10 No "personal rewards"

To my knowledge, no significant political or legislative decision has ever been influenced in the EU through bribery or extortion. The decision making process is such that it would be very difficult to bribe all those people that are involved. Moreover, both EU officials and elected politicians are relatively well paid and respect high moral standards. There are some rules but they are of little practical relevance. And while a good meal in a nice restaurant can certainly provide an agreeable climate for a discussion, it is ridiculous to believe that any decision maker could be bought in Brussels with such a meal.

In conclusion, my experience with being an EU representative of a company or of a sector organisation has always been positive and challenging. Doors are open if you knock on them in the right way, if you respect the written and unwritten rules and, also, if you are ready to bring something to the table.

I wrote in the beginning that things have changed over the time, and not always for the better for those who want to represent the legitimate interests of stakeholders. But this is life and progress. One has to adapt to new circumstances – and flexibility and adaptability is certainly one of the most important abilities of representatives and lobbyists.

4.2 Oliver Deiters, Managing Director of the DEKRA Representation to the European Union, Brussels

Lobbying – or the art of convincing others of my opinion

When I began representing the opinions of others to the decision makers in the European Commission and the Parliament in Brussels, I often asked myself questions such as the following:

...what exactly is "lobbying"?
...when am I successful?
...how exactly do you "lobby"?
...which concrete techniques and actions exist?
...which rules do I have to follow?
...how do I create an efficient network?
...can everybody do lobbying?
...are those people more successful, who already know lobbying from home?

So many questions. To be honest, I am still searching for the truth – even after 14 years! You could now ask yourself: "What kind of lobbyist is that who still has not found all the answers after 14 years?" I claim that most lobbyists in Brussels do not know the answers to the questions listed above.

Lobbying is not really taught as a university course. It is true that a lot has changed in Europe in recent years – but you cannot really learn how to lobby at universities and academies. So to speak, you learn how to lobby "on the job". In the following text, I will try to find a few answers to the questions above. In order to help answer the questions, I will make a comparison to the present-day centre of lobbying, namely Washington D.C.

In the U.S., lobbying per se constitutes a lawful opportunity available to interest groups to exert influence and to have an impact on policy. The right to lobby is implicitly derived from the First Amendment of the U.S. Constitution, which states "Congress shall make no law [...] abridging the freedom of speech or of the press; or the right of the people peaceably to assemble and to petition the Government for redress of grievances." The rationale of lobbyists in the US legislation process stems from the belief that a democratic society amid pluralistic and equitable intent of public representation does not necessarily guarantee equal access of individual opinion, and, hence, any tool to foster awareness of dissenting views and objectives ought to be allowed.

In contrast, opponents of lobbying, especially European scholars, generally believe that lobbying undermines the democratic principles of deriving and exercising public authority. They also entertain the notion that lobbyists would relegate democracy to the status of consumption good that could be sold. According to their view, lobbying means denying the principle of equal representation, which is the very purpose of representative democracy[105].

However, lobbying is an integrated part of the communication strategies and public affairs of various private and public actors: undertakings, groups, federations and associations but also regions or states.

The discussion on EU level regarding the regulation of the lobbyist profession comes at a time where experiences have shown to what extent interest representations participate in the European legislation process and thus mold the piece of legislation according to their particular interests. The role of lobbying within the legislation process on EU level has recently gained more importance in Brussels, at a similar degree in comparison with Washington D.C.

105 Jobst, Andreas: "Foreign Lobbying in the U.S. – A Latin American Perspective", London School of Economics and Political Science, 2002

Examining recent developments, it is obvious that lobbyists in Brussels have increasingly adopted not only the level of professionalism used in Washington D.C., but also the formal and informal rules and techniques which are used in the US in order to carry out successful lobbying[106].

There are several terms used to describe and define the activities of intentional political influence: lobbying, interest representation, public affairs, mobilisation, political pressure, etc. The word "lobbying" has acquired in time negative connotations, i.e. lobbying confers an unfair advantage on those that can afford to carry it out and therefore runs counter to the notion of democracy[107]. According to the definition of Warleigh and Fairbrass, "it ranges across lobbying, the exchange of information, alliance building, formal and informal contact, planned and unplanned relationships: in other words, all forms of interaction that are designed to advocate particular ideas, persuade the decision takers to adopt different positions or perspectives, and ultimately to influence policy"[108].

The institutional framework and the legislative process, both in the EU and in the US, are to a certain degree similar, however lobbying in the US is far more developed and publicly accepted than on European level.

Through the special responsibility of US Congressmen towards their constituencies, grassroots lobbying and electoral campaign funding have developed to special forms of interest representation. Also in the US interest organisation regarding non-profit organisations is significantly more present or visible than on European level, and especially regarding citizen groups, cause groups, profession groups and public interest groups. Furthermore, labour unions are relatively strongly represented, as well as so-called citizen groups, covering economic, occupational or other backgrounds and representing any type of citizen interest.

The European Union is a supranational organisation: its twenty-five Member States have conferred parts of their sovereign powers to the EU institutions. The Council of Ministers, composed of national representatives at ministerial level, exercises along with the European Parliament, legislative powers. The European Commission as driving force of European integration holds the right of initiative and vast executive powers. Finally, the European Court of Justice is the judicial power.

Due to its multilevel character, the EU legislation process provides for sufficient and ample intervening opportunities, so that interest representations can present their expertise, comments or

[106] For a more detailed approach see also Lahusen, Christian and Jauß, Claudia: "Lobbying als Beruf. Interessengruppen in der Europäischen Union", Nomos Verlag, Baden-Baden, 2001; [107] Warleigh, Alex and Fairbrass, Jenny: "Influence and Interests in the European Union: The New Politics of Persuasion and Advocacy", Europa Publications, London, 2002, p.2 et sqq.; [108] Idem, p.2

amendments in front of the European Commission, the European Parliament or the Council. Depending on the lobbying techniques and instruments chosen, such interventions can be carried out at different stages of the legislation process: in the primary stage of preparing and drafting the piece of legislation, during the official consultation procedures held either by the Commission or the Parliament, during the final adoption process or even during the implementation of the EU legislation on national level.

It has been often underlined, that a lobbyist has better chances of successfully achieving his strategic goals if he gets active at an early stage of the legislation process. At such a moment, he is able to examine the political scene and potential trends, make useful coalitions and establish contacts and networks. Once there are already more interest representatives active on the political arena[109], it will be harder to obtain access to policy makers and provide them with expertise.

This crucial issue of determining the perfect time when to lobby has been examined in the specialised literature. There are three different moments when a lobbyist can begin to act: the preventive lobbying, which aims to prevent or to postpone particular legislation before the call for legislative action even exists; the reaction lobbying means that the legislative proposal already exists and lobbying reacts to the legislative process, either in attempting to amend the proposal or to prevent it; and finally lobbying as action, referring to the need of legislation seen by a lobbyist and his actions to initiate the legislation considered necessary[110].

In this relationship it must be taken into consideration that lobbying the European institutions often means providing an exchange of information. The fundamental relationship between the interest representatives and the European institutions is one of exchange: the EU institutions seek information and expertise, interest groups seek influence. If they want to take influence, they have to provide information[111]. In contrast, US policy makers do not necessarily rely on outside information provided by interest groups, but instead assign research and preparatory work to their internal staff.

As the complexity of the legislative process has increased over time, and the number of political players involved with forming policy has also increased considerably, policy makers find themselves with highly complex and technical issues and less and less time to inform themselves and to understand them. Thus, interest groups help filling these informational gaps.

[109] Van Schendelen, p.131; [110] Bender and Reulecke 2003, p. 117
[111] See Bouwen 2002; Michalowitz 2005

One of the main roles of interest representatives in the EU is to provide policy makers with information and expertise so that they can decide how to vote and act on particular legislative issues[112]. These views of lobbyists as providers of information leave many likely possibilities for lobbyist action: in addition to technical expertise, interest representatives are able to provide political intelligence regarding especially possible effects of the legislation, but also linked services, including legislation drafting, legislative strategy planning, and speech writing.

Direct as well as indirect lobbying is comparably common both in Brussels and in Washington D.C. In order to maximize the effects of their lobbying activities, lobbyists often accompany their direct communication approach with instruments of indirect communication, for instance expertise, reports and surveys, campaigns, confer-ences and events.

When speaking of assessing the success of lobbyists, we first have to quantify the political influence lobbyists exert on policy makers. It is obvious that lobbyists, both in the EU and US, play some role in influencing and shaping legislation, even if the literature does not agree on the magnitude of that role[113].

Regarding the possibility of assessing lobbying success, empirical findings suggest that EU lobbyists might have less influence on European decision makers than assumed and also less influence than their colleagues in Washington D.C. In the European Union, political influence depends on the political will of decision makers. According to Michalowitz, most empirical studies of EU lobbying limit themselves to describing lobbying cases, but stop short of determining actual influence gained by lobbying. EU lobbying researchers seem to assume that the empirical evidence demonstrating influence of lobbying groups in other political systems, notably in the US, is a sufficient indicator to assume that the same holds true for EU lobbying[114].

In other words, US lobbyists are more successful in shaping US legislation than their colleagues in the European Union. However, the assessment of lobbying success still remains difficult, since it relies on the definition of strategic goals and desired outcomes. If this definition is rather vague and the goals and outcomes are established for a medium to long term, the evaluation of the achievements is also rather vague and undetermined.

The present paper examined first the external circumstances of lobbying, focusing on the political, administrative and institutional environment and enhancing in its comparative approach the characteristic differences between the US and the EU. This comparative

[112] See Michalowitz 2005; Milbrath 1963; R. Smith 1984; Schlozman and Tierney 1986; Van Schendelen 2004
[113] See Lowi 1979; Milbrath 1963; Segal, Cameron, and Cover 1992; Smith 2000; Smith 1995; Wright 1996
[114] Michalowitz 2005, p. 2

view is important since it presents the special circumstances in which lobbyists react not only to the demands and constraints of policy makers, but also to the surrounding political environment and to common practices. Thus, the entire political environment shapes the approach lobbyists take when influencing policy makers.

Although lobbyists can choose their strategy in influencing decision makers and thus achieving their clients' goals freely, they are often influenced themselves by characteristics and constraints of the relevant playing field. The best example in this sense is the most appropriate channel of influence which a lobbyist can choose, according to its own opinion and search work. In the EU, the European channel (through Euro-federations and associations or even through direct contact with European policy makers) is more often used than the national channel (through national decision-makers or representations of interest). In the US, lobbyists rather approach Congressmen through their constituencies, so to speak through a local channel. Thus, the comparison of different lobbying activities and the evaluation of success must also take into consideration such external factors.

Since lobbying success does not always lead to the adoption or prevention of a piece of legislation, it is difficult to evaluate and compare. The examination of the degree of success of a lobbyist must take into consideration all his activities and assess the techniques used in relationship with the final outcome. Monitoring, research and information are a necessary prerequisite for any lobbying activity in order to evaluate the political scene, the policy makers and potential allies and/or competitors. Furthermore, a detailed and periodic monitoring might show potential political trends even before the actual need for legislating has occurred. Only when this preliminary phase of preparation is soundly and comprehensively fulfiled, can a lobbyist be sure to prepare and use the adequate lobbying techniques and instruments and thus to obtain its strategic goals.

Furthermore, the strategic objectives either set up by the lobbyist himself or by the clients he is representing often differ in subject and content: legislation monitoring and research work can be easily evaluated, but politically influencing decision makers in the long term is more difficult to determine at a certain moment and to objectively prove. It is also difficult to asses the impact of information campaigns or publicity events on the agenda setting and finally on the decision makers. Publicity always draws the attention of policy makers, but it is not easy to establish to what extent they let themselves be influenced in the legislation process.

Also, as long as the interviewers do not apply parameters of general applicability in both the EU and US, the success assessment of US and EU lobbyists is hard to compare.

5. Associations

Philippe de Buck, Secretary General of UNICE, the Confederation of European Businesses, Brussels

Putting Competitiveness on the map

The competitiveness of the European economy has always been UNICE's top priority. In advance of the European Council in Lisbon in March 2000, the Presidents of UNICE, at that time from 35 business federations in 27 countries, urged the European Council to „speed up economic and structural reforms in the EU and to boost European employment, innovation and entrepreneurship". UNICE President Georges Jacobs stressed the urgency of reforms „to enable Europe to catch up and be more competitive in the new and fast-moving e-economy". Therefore, the business community's assessment of what is now known as the Lisbon agenda was broadly positive. In a first reaction on 24 March 2000, Georges Jacobs stated that the business community was „happy with this new momentum in the EU to tackle the high unemployment rates through economic and structural reforms". „Reforms are urgent" said UNICE and „a rapid implementation of the outcome of Lisbon is absolutely necessary to enable Europe to catch up in the new and fast-moving economy". In particular, the setting of concrete targets and timetables was welcome to reach these objectives. However, UNICE urged national governments „to impose shorter and sufficiently ambitious deadlines". In any event, after that promising start, achieving has proved harder than setting them. For UNICE, competitiveness remained the most important issue to achieve the Lisbon goals. The following are milestones in that process.

5.1 "Free Gulliver!" – First Competitiveness Day on 14 November 2003

The purpose of this event was to demonstrate the need for more competitiveness in Europe. Business leaders from all over Europe shared their first-hand experience about what is hampering business activity and what needs to be changed. Under the leitmotiv "Release companies' potential – Free Gulliver!" several hundred entrepreneurs and business leaders from all over Europe came together in Brussels on 14 November 2003 at the first UNICE Competitiveness Day. They discussed Europe's competitiveness challenges and necessary actions to be taken to relaunch the EU economy with high-level politicians, including Italian Prime Minister Silvio Berlusconi and Italian Minister for Productive Activities Antonio Marzano, representing the Italian Presidency of the Council of the European Union, as well as Enterprise Commissioner Erkki Liikanen, and Irish Minister for European Affairs Dick Roche. The essence of all appeals was concentrated in the "Manifesto for Competitiveness" which was handed over to Silvio Berlusconi, President of the European Council at that time. It gave a clear message of what policy-makers were expected to do. But UNICE President Jürgen Strube, successor of Georges Jacobs, also gave a clear message to business leaders: if they really wanted to make a difference, they all needed to become ambassadors for competitiveness. This also included convincing European society that entrepreneurial spirit and energy was the only way out of its current problems. The Conference expressed strong hopes for the so-called Competitiveness Council, which it hoped would embody a new integrated strategy for competitiveness. But that made it necessary for this gathering of Member States' governments to become a body for enacting the will of all Member States to improve business conditions in Europe. As a policy priority, the business community committed strongly to support this Council formation, and the national ministers who were members of it.

As a follow up to this first UNICE demonstration, in March 2004, UNICE and its member federations published the "Competitiveness Action Plan", a compilation of actions needed at national level for each of the 5 priority areas identified in the "Manifesto for Competitiveness". One year before the mid-term review of the Lisbon Strategy, UNICE already asked for a stronger commitment at national level.

5.2 Presentation of Business vision for Europe on 9 September 2004

When José Manuel Barroso was appointed new President of the European Commission, UNICE called upon the new College of Commissioners to steer a clear course towards progressive, economic reform-oriented policy. UNICE had high expectations that Mr Barroso would be a real „Lisbon" President. He had rightly pointed out that globalisation meant facing up to competition in open, global markets – and therefore the European business community expected from the new Commission that they would give the appropriate competitiveness-oriented answers. To feed our call for competitiveness, UNICE elaborated the UNICE Business Vision – Growth, Jobs and Prosperity which outlined the policy areas where progress with ambitious reforms was key. This document laid out the vision European business had for Europe. It was targeted on the members of the new Commission to be appointed at that time, the newly elected members of the European Parliament, and the Member States' governments. "What you will decide during your mandate between 2004 and 2009 is key for the future of each of our fellow citizens. Therefore, we expect a clear strategy focused on competitiveness, realistic in its objectives and with a strong commitment to implement decisions already taken. Furthermore, your policy approach must include an in-depth communication strategy convincing European citizens, governments – all stakeholders – that better competitiveness is the only way to more growth, jobs and prosperity" highlighted UNICE President Jürgen Strube and Secretary General Philippe de Buck in the document. UNICE urged political decision-makers to be the engine for change in Europe, all the more important in light of the enlargement on 1 May 2004, and future enlargements. In the Business Vision for Europe – growth, jobs and prosperity, UNICE identified six priorities:

• release entrepreneurial energy
• boost innovation
• unleash the internal market of 25+
• make environmental policy more effective and efficient
• foster international trade and investment
• improve the functioning of the labour market and social systems.

UNICE also reiterated the ultimate goal of the Lisbon Strategy, which was to achieve sustainable well-being in Europe. To make its three pillars – economic, social and environmental – mutually reinforcing, Europe had to recognise that the basis for sustainable development was sound economic growth. Europe would only secure sound economic growth if its companies were competitive. In the interest of society as a whole, the new European institutions had to focus all their policies on the objective of enhancing competitiveness in Europe.

5.3 "Play to win" – Second UNICE Competitiveness Day on 9 December 2004

Three months later, hundreds of business people from all over Europe again followed UNICE's call to demonstrate for a competitive Europe at the second Competitiveness Day on 9 December 2004 in the Brussels EP Hemicycle. Under the Chairmanship of UNICE President Jürgen Strube, business leaders discussed the need for economic reform with high-level political decision-makers. Participants included the President of the European Parliament Josep Borrell, Commission President José Manuel Barroso, Dutch Minister of Economics Laurens Jan Brinkhorst, and ECB President Jean-Claude Trichet. The event took place close to the mid-term of the Lisbon timeframe, a moment when the new EU institutions could provide a turning point for the second half of the Lisbon implementation. The participants discussed the report on the status of the Lisbon strategy published by the Wim Kok expert group some weeks earlier. Like UNICE, it found that implementation was unsatisfactory. This diagnosis of the current delivery gap, together with its reaffirmation of the validity of the Lisbon strategy, and its recommendation that Member States should take ownership of the Lisbon implementation process, made the Kok report a useful input. The national record for implementing the Lisbon reforms had been very different across Member States. The national Lisbon plans would make national governments accountable for their reform efforts vis-à-vis national parliaments, stakeholders, and citizens. UNICE President Jürgen Strube rejected all talk about postponing the deadline for achievement of Lisbon. In addition, European and national legislators had to refrain from overburdening the Lisbon agenda with additional objectives. It was to focus clearly on the Lisbon goal of faster European GDP growth, created by enhanced competitiveness, as the basis for Europe's social model and environmental policies. A more positive attitude and a conducive environment for business could release Europe's growth potential, currently around 2% against a figure of closer to 4% in the USA. Faster economic growth would create a virtuous circle generating jobs and allowing improved social and environmental standards.

The conference gave a positive message: European companies had the potential for world-class performance if their potential was released. This potential was illustrated by the leitmotiv "Play to win": given the right conditions, and with a determined effort by all stakeholders, Europe's economy was capable of producing a winning performance.

5.4 Refocus of Lisbon Strategy in Spring 2005

A few months later, in spring 2005, the European Commission published its communication for the 2005 Spring EU Council. The College proposed refocusing the Lisbon Strategy on growth and employment, given the current situation in Europe of low growth, an ageing population and intensifying global competition. In a first public reaction, UNICE strongly supported this proposal. Apart from acting in a focused way, a crucial success factor for the Lisbon Strategy remained the commitment of national governments to reform. The proposed partnership for growth and jobs had to be extended to national actors. National action programmes, to be developed by the Member States, would be the centerpiece for the follow-up of national action. At the request of UNICE, member federations had already launched their own national initiatives for competitiveness, urging their governments to start or accelerate national reform programmes. The reaction to the following Spring Summit on 23 March 2005 was more ambivalent. UNICE had expected a relaunch of the Lisbon Strategy in that meeting, in order to create confidence for citizens and businesses. Unfortunately, the European Council had not taken that opportunity. Nevertheless, as most of the work ahead would have to come from the Member States, UNICE trusted that the 2005-2008 National Action Programmes agreed at the summit would help identify priority actions for reform.

5.5 Crossing Frontiers – Third Competitiveness Day on 20 October 2005

Following its new tradition, UNICE again mobilised more than one thousand people, mostly business representatives, to participate in Brussels on 20 October at the 3rd UNICE Competitiveness Day "Crossing Frontiers". They debated the challenges of globalisation with the President of the European Parliament, Josep Borrell, European Commission President José Manuel Barroso, and Barry Gardiner, UK Under-Secretary of State, representing the British Presidency. With the revision of the Growth and Jobs Strategy, Europe had seen competitiveness moving up the agenda. It was now the moment to keep up the pressure to ensure that necessary reforms were implemented. If Europe was to come to grips with and successfully adapt to the challenges of globalisation, demography and new technology, EU policies had to be revised in a way that helped companies: competitiveness had to be the central concern steering trade policy, industrial policy, and labour market policy. UNICE identified four key priorities where initiatives at both national and European level are essential:

- unleash the internal market
- modernise the European social model
- get a deal on the EU budget
- sort out the institutional deadlock

The new President of UNICE, Ernest-Antoine Seillière, deplored a missing sense of urgency: "We cannot act on a basis of 'business as usual': failure to tackle our challenges satisfactorily will not be without consequences for Europe, not least because there is a risk that the sense of drifting without clear purpose may turn into a questioning of the entire European project!"

5.6 Spring Council in March 2006

Ahead of the Spring European Council, the Commission's Progress Report on the European Growth and Jobs Strategy presented on 25 January 2006 again offered a good basis for policy makers throughout Europe to deliver on the Strategy for Growth and Jobs. The report made an assessment of the 25 National Reform Programmes in which each Member State put forward its planned and current national reform actions. It stressed the strengths but also weaknesses of each National Reform Programme. Many of the programmes lacked ambition when it came to concrete implementation of the announced reforms. UNICE expressed hope that the Spring European Council would take these assessments seriously into account and ask for improvements to the reform programmes where necessary. The Commission and the

Council were asked to develop resolute governance mechanisms to monitor national reforms. As after every Spring Summit, the Council produced a thick 35-page paper of conclusions on economic reform. They addressed the important economic policy challenges Europe was currently facing. One positive element was the emphasis on implementing National Reform Programmes and the recognition that they could include more specific targets and timetables. "But will they just turn out to be a report on yet another annual discussion on growth and jobs, or will they mark the beginning of a real commitment from political leaders? UNICE calls with all its might for the latter", President Seillière reacted in a public statement.

5.7 "Why do companies care about Europe?" – Unice Day 2006

At this year's edition on 17 October 2006 in Brussels, the European business community asked companies whether and why they should care about Europe. The conference debated the current deficiencies of Europe, but also the great benefits European integration has offered to citizens and companies. Hundreds of business people questioned the efficiency and the objectives of Europe and its companies once more. Among the participants were Matti Vanhanen, Prime Minister of Finland, the President of the European Parliament Josep Borrell, President of the European Commission José Manuel Barroso and his fellow Commissioners Günter Verheugen, Charlie McCreevy, Joaquín Almunia, Peter Mandelson, Dalia Grybauskaité, the WTO Director General Pascal Lamy, and high-level business representatives including Jorma Ollila, Chairman of Nokia, and Chairman of Shell, Jean-Martin Folz, Chairman of the Managing Board of PSA Peugeot Citroën, Confindustria President Luca Cordero di Montezemolo, BDI President Jürgen Thumann and MEDEF President Laurence Parisot.

The European business community will demonstrate its commitment to Europe and call for strong reforms, indispensable for the well-being of the European project.

6. NGOs

6.1 Willy Fautré, Director of Human Rights without Frontiers Int., Brussels

In 1989, a number of human rights defenders founded an NGO called "Bruxelles Droits de l'Homme/ Brussels Human Rights/ Brüssel Menschenrechte", later renamed to Droits de l'homme sans frontières. The organisation has gradually expanded into Human Rights Without Frontiers International (HRWF Int.) to embrace its branch offices in Belgium, China, USA, and Nepal as well as its associate members in Armenia (Pro-Democracy Association), Bulgaria (Tolerance Foundation), Georgia (Human Rights Information and Documentation Centre), Iraq (Assyrian Aid Society), Japan (Life Funds for North Korean Refugees), Russia, and South Korea. Since 1997, the Belgian branch of HRWF Int. has been an associate member of the International Helsinki Federation for Human Rights.

Crucial to the success of any advocacy activities is the strength of NGOs to mobilise enough political energy and will and their ability to link up with other organisations in cohesive networks, which have sufficient credibility and power to spur actions on particular issues.

Our work on North Korean human rights and refugees is one case from the most recent activities of HRWF Int. that can best illustrate our advocacy philosophy and approach:

Human Rights without Frontiers Int. (HRWF Int.) launched its project on North Korean Human Rights and Refugees in 2001, in the wake of the publishing of Les aquariums de Pyongyang: Dix ans au goulag nord-coréen by the French author Pierre Rigoulot, one of the members of the HRWF Int. Board of Directors. The book describes the life of Kang Chol-Hwan who has spent ten years in Yodok camp and is considered one of the first published works bringing light to the fact that there are camps in existence in North Korea.

The project gained momentum with the process of collecting information on human rights in North Korea and the situation of North Korean refugees fleeing into China. Throughout this process, HRWF Int. identified reliable partners and organisations in the region working on this particular subject and expanded its network for obtaining trustworthy information. The collection of personal interviews in the field and testimonies of people who have suffered in camps or have witnessed the suffering of other people provided a solid basis of information and helped us articulate specific issues at stake, which allowed us to move on to the next stage of our advocacy cycle – the communication. The publication of an article in the New York Times in June 2002, reprinted in the International Herald Tribune[115] few days later, about the results of HRWF Int. fact-finding mission on practices of infanticide and forced abortions in North Korean camps, provided a strong impetus to this stage of our project, as the interest in North Korean human rights grew quickly and attracted much attention on the side of international media, NGOs and intergovernmental organisations. Meetings, interviews and small-scale hearings organised by HRWF Int. for Members of the European Parliament, members of national parliaments as well as officials of UN agencies, the EU institutions and other intergovernmental organisations opened up new channels for communication on issues related to North Korean human rights and refugees that have previously not existed.

In March 2006, the communication stage of our project was brought to a higher level of success when a wide-scale public hearing was organised at the European Parliament under the aegis of the Alliance of Liberals and Democrats for Europe (ALDE).

The attention given to North Korean human rights and refugees spurred action on the policy level. In two successive years, at sessions of the UN Commission on Human Rights in Geneva in 2003 and 2004, the European Union acted as the main initiator and sponsor of two resolutions dealing with North Korean human rights. These resolutions were adopted, as a result of which the position of Special Rapporteur on the situation of human rights in the Democratic People's Republic of Korea was established. Prof. Vitit Muntarbhorn from Thailand was appointed Special Rapporteur for a period of one year to study the human rights situation in North Korea and to report his findings and analysis to respective UN bodies and institutions. In November 2005, the UN General Assembly adopted a resolution on the situation of human rights in the Democratic People's Republic of Korea, urging its government to fully respect human rights and fundamental freedoms.

Thus far, the project can be considered successful on several stages: agenda-setting, changes in the discourse of international organisations and changes in institutional procedures. Human rights in North Korea and the plight of North Koreans fleeing their country have generated enough interest to be an issue of public debates. The flow of information providing testimonies and personal accounts of those who have been affected by the violation of human rights has created a certain momentum leading to changes in the discourse of international organisations such as the European Union and the United Nations. The UN General Assembly resolution and the two resolutions of the UN Commission on Human Rights, which were drafted, tabled and sponsored by the European Union, are a clear demonstration of these changes. The establishment of the position of Special Rapporteur on the situation of human rights in the Democratic People's Republic of Korea is representative of changes in institutional procedures, which are needed as mechanisms for flow of information and leverage. Tangible changes in state's behaviour towards full respect for human rights and fundamental freedoms in conformity with international norms and standards are slow to come. Nevertheless, the small steps along the way are representative of the cohesion of transnational advocacy networks, which we are part of, and of their ability to mobilise their strength and energy around issues that threaten to undermine the validity of international human rights norms.

So, from the inception of HRWF Int., the main focus of our activities has been monitoring, research, and analysis in the field of human rights as well as promotion of democracy and the rule of law on national and international level. In these endeavors, we have been guided by the understanding that it is not sufficient for international norms and standards in the field of human rights to be approved and adopted by governments. States enjoy different levels of approximation to democratic development and the rule of law and human rights norms do not always have a "taken-for-granted" quality. In many cases, they still need to undergo a long, and sometimes painful, process of socialisation in order to become integrated into state policies. The success of this process would be predicated, among other things, on the strength of non-governmental human rights networks to instigate changes towards human rights promotion.

We also work on the assumption that ideas, and not only state interests and positions, matter in international relations. In this respect, international human rights instruments can be seen as representing the ultimate expression of collective ideas of social justice. As such, we consider their implementation to be of utmost importance as an overarching framework for the ideas of liberty, democracy, the rule of law.

Within this context, HRWF Int. has adopted an approach to human rights promotion, which is wider in scope than lobbying on a specific human right. Our emphasis is on human rights advocacy, which we understand as a process, through which we bring new ideas, norms and discourses into policy debates and promote norm implementation by pressuring target actors to adopt new policies and by monitoring compliance with international standards.

In pursuit of this overarching objective, the HRWF Int. has been using three main strategies: information, communication, and leverage. Gathering trustworthy information of situations of human rights violations is essential in constructing a solid case which merits attention and advocacy. Our strength is in having access to diverse sources of information being part of wider advocacy networks with assured flow of information bringing in not only facts but also testimonies of people whose lives have been affected. On the level of communication, we try to generate attention to issues at stake, alert policy makers to long-term implications of specific human rights abuses and open up channels of communication on the international arena as means of gaining attention. New issues can be brought up for public debate through various advocacy techniques: media attention, debates, hearings, and larger conferences. Though information gathering and communication are an important part of our advocacy campaigns, the crucial strategic step is to gain enough influence to induce changes in state positions and policies. In this respect, we seek to bring the human rights record of targeted countries to the light of international scrutiny using moral leverage, which some observers have called the "mobilisation of shame". Exploring different avenues of communication with international organisations or individual countries, we seek to put forward solid arguments on the link between human rights issues on one side and economic aid or other forms of cooperation, on the other.

Part of our advocacy cycle is devoted to formulating issues and identifying possible "target" loci of advocacy, which are primarily in the domain of international organisations. The United Nations, the European Union, the Council of Europe and the Organisation for Security and Co-operation in Europe (OSCE) are the main venues for targeted and structured human rights advocacy activities.

The European Union is an important international actor and human rights have become an integral and important part of its external relations. The principles of liberty, democracy, the rule of law and the respect for human rights are goals of the foreign and security policy of the European Union and underpin its co-operation with third countries. In this respect, the EU institutions – the European Commission, the European Parliament, and the Council of the European Union – are crucial to human rights promotion worldwide.

The effectiveness of our advocacy activities is difficult to assess due to the long period over which real changes may occur. Instead, we try to measure relative success on different stages of the advocacy cycle: 1) agenda setting, i.e. whether a specific issue has generated enough interest to be publicly debated; 2) changes in the discourse of states and international organisations; 3) changes in institutional procedures; 4) changes in policies; 5) changes in behaviour of states in conformity with human rights norms and standards.

6.2 Rev Dieter Heidtmann, Executive Secretary of the Church and Society Commission of the Conference of European Churches and
Rev Rüdiger Noll, Director of the Church and Society Commission of the Conference of European Churches and Associate General Secretary of the Conference of European Churches, Brussels

Lobbying or Advocacy?

It does not go without saying, that a handbook on lobbying the European Union institutions should include a chapter on the churches[116]. There are more than a few people who would argue that in modern societies, religion belongs to the private sphere of a person and should be limited in its influence on the public sector. Not the least due to a growing visibility of a fundamentalist type of religion and the religious connotations used to "justify" the terrorist attacks of 9/11, an increasing number of people regard religion rather as a part of the problem than as a part of the solution for present day conflicts.

This argument, however, neglects that even in secularising and pluralistic societies, as found in most European countries, faith and religion are and remain determining factors in people's lives[117]. Therefore, to exclude religion from the public discourse in civil society or from the dialogue with political decision makers would be illogical. It could even have counterproductive effects and play into the hands of fundamentalists, who would seek other ways of making themselves heard. Religion is an indispensable element in modern societies. In its enlightened and non-fundamentalist form, it requires the separation of church and state as well as a pluralism of positions and life stances in modern societies. It supports the fundamental pillars of modern societies, such as democracy, the protection of human rights and the rule of law.

Limiting religion to the private sphere also neglects how much religion and churches contribute to the fabric of society and its present

[116] This article draws largely on the experiences of the Conference of European Churches (CEC) and its 125 member churches from the Anglican, Old-Catholic, Orthodox, and Protestant tradition. The main mandate of CEC is to strengthen the unity of the churches and to support their common witness as churches in society. For further information on CEC consult its website www.cec-kek.org. The article is therefore written from the perspective of Christian Churches in Europe, which does not exclude similar approaches and experiences of other religious communities and communities of conviction, with which CEC cooperates closely.
[117] Cf. the results of the most recent European value studies as summarized in: Hermann Denz (Ed.), Die europäische See-le. Leben und Glauben in Europa, Wien (Czernin) 2002; Ulrich H.J. Körtner, Wiederkehr der Religion? Das Christentum zwischen neuer Spiritualität und Gottvergessenheit, Gütersloh (Gütersloher Verlagshaus) 2006. Cf. also: Grace Davie, Religion in Modern Europe. A Memory Mutates, Oxford (University Press) 2000.

day values. It neglects the contribution of religion to conflict prevention and non-violent ways of conflict management[118]. Governments
use churches to distribute a considerable amount of their development
aid and to care for victims of present developments, such as the unem-
ployed and migrants. In many European countries, churches are major
providers of social services. They run kindergartens, schools, hospitals,
homes for elderly people, soup kitchens, and support people excluded
from equal opportunities in society. For the churches, being engaged in
society in the form of social work and advocacy for the excluded and
marginalised is a constitutive element of their religious practice.

Nevertheless, it seems strange for them to be called "lobbyists". For
Europeans, the term "lobbyist" often has the negative connotation of
trying to influence political structures for one's own interests, in particular for one's own economic profit. However, churches and religious
communities do regard themselves as part of the non-profit sector, the
civil society[119], striving for the "common good". Many of the 125 member churches of the Conference of European Churches would even not
be happy with the label "civil society", because of their transcendent
dimension, which determines their aims, visions and objectives as well
as the contents and the style of their contribution. In their relation to
the European institutions, they are part of civil society, though a distinct
part. The European Union, in its law making capacity, determining people's lives just like any state, needs the participation and contribution of
interest groups such as civil society organisations and the churches. In
a time of a growing gap between people and political structures and an
increasing mistrust in the political process, this is even more important.

Case Study 1: The Treaty Establishing a Constitution for Europe

Monitoring the Convention on the Future of Europe and subsequent intergovernmental negotiation rounds, which developed the Treaty Establishing
a Constitution for Europe (further on referred to as: Constitutional Treaty),
was the biggest and most intensive monitoring operation with regard to
the European Institutions in which the Conference of European Churches
(CEC) was involved.

How did it all begin? When the Heads of State and Government of the
EU member countries met for the European Council in December 2001, the
crisis of the European Union had already become evident. The European
Council in Laeken (Belgium) identified three challenges: the democratic
challenge and the need to bring the EU closer to its citizens; the definition
of Europe's role in a globalised world; and meeting the expectations of

[118] In the recent past, religion has indeed been involved in both ways in conflict situations: it has been misused to exacerbate conflicts and it has made decisive contributions to mediate in conflict situations and work for a sustainable peace and reconciliation in post-conflict situations. Cf. R. Scott Appleby, The Ambivalence of the Sacred, Religion, Violence, and Reconciliation, London, Boulder, New York, Oxford (Rowman and Littlefield Publishers, Inc) 2000.; [119] Cf. David Herbert, Religion and Civil Society, Rethinking Public Religion in the Contemporary World, Burlington (Ashgate Publishing Company) 2004.

European Union citizens. A major issue behind many of these challenges was, however, the issue of the identity of the European Union and a lack of a vision. The common vision of the founders of the European Institutions (peace and prosperity in Europe) had faded away and individual governments used the European Union just to get the best deal for themselves.

In order to break this vicious circle, the European Council established, for the second time in its history, a Convention, a body alongside the existing institutional frame-work. The Convention with its 105 members was meant to guarantee the broadest possible and most representative participation from national as well European decision-making bodies. The Convention adopted as its main task the development of a Constitutional Treaty addressing the various challenges. In effect, it had only 16 months to draft a text of such importance. The Convention began its work in March 2002 with a period of listening and collecting data before entering into a stage of drafting in December.

For European churches, being committed to the European integration process, the work of the Convention and the prospects of a constitution-like text opened the possibility to participate in the process and to bring forward some of their main concerns with regard to developments in Europe. From the very beginning of the Convention's work, the Conference of European Churches advocated for

- the European Union to be not only an economic space, but a value based community
- the EU Charter on Fundamental Rights to become a legally binding text included in the Constitutional Treaty
- the social dimension to be an integral part of any European Union policy
- democratic structures and mechanisms for people's participation and involvement
- a right balance between the competences of the Union and member states
- Europe assuming its role and responsibility in a globalised world.

In addition, the churches lobbied for two issues addressing the relations between religious communities and the European Union:

- Up until now, there is no legal basis for the relationships between religious communities and the institutions of the European Union. Therefore the Conference of European Churches, together with the Roman Catholic Commission of Bishops' Conferences of the European Community (COMECE)[120] lobbied for a "structural dialogue" to be recognised in the Treaty.

- The Amsterdam Treaty of the European Union recognised, in an appended Declaration (No. 11), that the European Union respects and does not prejudice the status of churches and religious associations in member states. This stipulation was to be made an integral part of the Constitutional Treaty.

These issues were submitted with very detailed suggestions (sometimes even drafted text) to the Convention at several stages in the process, taking into account the processes and developments in the Convention itself. Within CEC, the content of these submissions was drafted by several existing and ad-hoc working groups and adopted by the Executive Committee of the Church and Society Commission.

From the very beginning, CEC together with COMECE, monitored every single session of the Convention and several sessions of its sub-committees with a special emphasis on the churches' own interests. In the first instance, the member churches of CEC were sent an information folder. After each session of the Convention, CEC and COMECE produced their own minutes and briefing papers[121], which were presented orally to briefing sessions in Brussels and sent to an ever-growing list of email contacts from member churches and interested people. To inform their own constituency became an important feature of the process and the interplay between national churches and their respective governments, and a European umbrella organisation such as CEC proved to be of utmost importance in the final stages of the adoption process.

Beyond informing its own constituency, the Conference of European Churches used press releases and public statements in order to inform a broader public and to ensure transparency about its concerns and sub-missions.

In monitoring the Convention, contacts to the Presidium of the Convention, to its Secretariat and to a high number of individual members of the Convention were established. These contacts allowed for the exchange of information and views, as well as for discussing the respective issues addressed by the Convention and the churches.

In the early phase of the Convention's work (listening phase), CEC submitted a general and public statement[122] to the Convention highlighting its issues and concerns. This was followed by a public Hearing of the Convention for civil society organisations in June 2002. The then Director of CEC's Church and Society Commission was selected by the communities of faith and conviction to present a joint statement at the Hearing.

The working style of the Convention changed considerably when it moved from the listening period to the drafting stage. In autumn/winter

[121] Now published in book form: The European Convention. The evolution of a Constitution for Europe, Joint documentation by the Church and Society Commission of the Conference of European Churches, the Evangelical Church in Germany and the Commission of the Bishops' Conferences of the European Community, Brussels 2003.
[122] Submissions to the Convention as well as press releases of the Conference of European Churches referred to in this text could be found on CEC's website: www.cec-kek.org. Submissions to the Convention were also posted on the Convention's public Forum website.

2002, the Convention published a first annotated table of contents of the Constitutional Treaty. From then on, the submissions of the Conference of European Churches (often joint statements with COMECE) tried to be more precise, referring to specific articles of the text and offering, wherever possible, language for the respective articles to be drafted. Timing proved to be of utmost importance, i.e. making suggestions at the appropriate time to the right bodies. In January 2002, CEC submitted two proposals to the Convention; one on social issues and another on the legal status of churches.

Especially the submission on social issues might serve as an example. Quite a number of Convention members wanted to see social issues and policies prominently addressed in the Constitutional Treaty. Therefore, they suggested a Sub-Committee on socials issues to be established. This was long refused by the Leadership of the Convention with reference to the fact that social issues are not a main competence of the European Union. Representatives of CEC spoke to many of the Convention members who had asked for a Sub-Committee on Social Issues, and supported their view by informing member churches and a broader public.

The Sub-Committee was finally established in December 2002. It was expected to report back in February 2003, in only two months time, which included a major holiday period. CEC immediately established a Task-Force on Social Issues with members of its constituency and representatives of church-related service providers. It was this group, which in relating the concerns of the churches to the concerns of Convention members drafted CEC's submission on social issues. It promoted several values and objectives of the European Union to be included in the first articles of the Constitutional Treaty, which were not yet mentioned in the annotated table of contents published by the Convention. The main concern of CEC, however, was to make the social dimension an integral part of any EU policy.

In the end, many of the values and objectives promoted by CEC jointly with other civil society organisations found their way into Articles I-2 and I-3 of the Constitutional Treaty. One of the last articles, which found its way into the Treaty as part of the inter-governmental negotiations after the Convention, now stipulates, that the European Union in all its policies "shall take into account ... the guarantee of adequate social protection". (Art III-117) And finally, Article I-52 includes Declaration 11 of the Amsterdam Treaty as well as a commitment for an "open, transparent and regular dialogue" of the European Union with churches and communities of faith and conviction.

One of the most heated debates in the Convention, and thereafter, centered around a reference to God or the Christian roots of Europe in the Preamble of the Constitutional Treaty. Member churches of CEC were divided on this issue. While a majority of churches would have liked a reference to

God in the Preamble in order to recognise that life and human dignity is not human made, others argued that a secular text does not need a reference to God, and a reference to Christianity would need to do justice to the presence of other religions and life stances in modern Europe. After intensive discussions in decision-making bodies of CEC, several formulations were offered to the Convention and EU Presidencies as "desirable options". It was clear, however, that a reference to God or Christianity in a Preamble would not be an alternative to a legally binding Article I-52.

The important role of civil society organisations as well as of the churches and religious communities was clearly recognised by the European Commission in its 2001 White Paper of the European Commission on "European Governance"[123] which reads: "Civil society plays an important role in giving voice to the concerns of citizens and delivering services that meet people's needs. Churches and religious communities have a particular contribution to make. The organisations which make up civil society mobilise people and support, for instance, for those suffering from exclusion or discrimination"[124].

In a similar way, the Treaty Establishing a Constitution for Europe, which was adopted by the Heads of State and Government of EU member states in October 2004 and still awaits ratification, recognises the specific contribution of civil society and the communities of faith and conviction as a distinct part of civil society. It is out of this conviction that Article I-47 (2) reads: "The institutions [of the European Union] shall maintain an open, transparent and regular dialogue with representative associations of civil society". In the Treaty, churches and communities of faith and conviction are related to, but not just subsumed under the term "civil society". This becomes evident in that a special Article (I-52) in the Treaty deals with the churches and communities of faith and conviction, though employing almost the same language as in Article I-47(2). Article I-52(3) refers to the "identity" and "specific contribution" of churches and communities of faith and conviction: "Recognising their identity and their specific contribution, the Union shall maintain an open, transparent and regular dialogue with these churches and organisations."

But what is it that constitutes the identity and the specific contribution of churches? Some features of churches might help answer this question. These features might also be looked upon as strategic advantages of churches, which make their contribution in the dialogue with the European institutions so valuable:

[123] COM(2001) 428 final.
[124] For the reference to the particular contribution of churches and religious communities also see Footnote 8 on page 9 of the White Paper.

- Churches reflect and act on the basis of visions and value systems, which are not human-made and self-centered, but which derive from the divine revelation as expressed in the Bible. In addressing today's challenges, this divine revelation is not neutral in its approach: it commits the churches to a preferential option for the poor and marginalised in our societies, to non-violence and reconciliation as well as to the protection of the environment and the responsibility for future generations[125]. Being rooted in the will of God, the transcendent dimension serves as a critical corrective to many present trends as well as a self-critical corrective for the churches themselves. The churches' contribution does not depend on fashionable opinions. Thus, the churches have the potential to serve as a long-term conscience in society.
- Churches are organised on a local, national, regional (European) and global level. It is in the interplay between these different levels, that coherent and sustainable policies addressing local, national, regional and global political structures can be developed. Churches think globally and can act on the appropriate level.
- Through the local congregations and church-related grassroot communities, the churches are connected to the people, their day-to-day realities and living experiences. This particularly enables the churches to be advocates of the people, especially the marginalised and excluded.
- People from all walks of life participate in the churches: men and women, young and old, people of different ethnic origins and social backgrounds. Thus, churches represent a diversity of people and approaches. Issues presented by churches to governments and the European institutions have already gone through a broad reflection process, including major sectors of society.
- Compared to various "single issue organisations" in civil society, churches cover the whole range of issues which affect people's lives. Thus, the churches have less of a tendency to overemphasise the urgency and importance of one issue over and against any other. They are well placed to address the complexity and balance of today's challenges.

With the exception of the transcendent dimension, none of the above-mentioned features alone, distinguishes the churches from other civil society organisations. This is why churches and civil society organisations can often work together towards the "common good". But it is all of the above features together and their interplay which constitute the special identity and the special contribution of the churches.

In 1989 (in Basel) and 1997 (in Graz), European churches organised two European Ecumenical Assemblies with several hundred delegates and several thousand participants. Twice, after the many preparatory attempts to address present challenges from a Christian and biblical perspective. Cf. Peace with Justice. The official documentation of the European Ecumenical Assembly Basel, Switzerland, 15–21 May, 1989, Geneva 1989: Reconciliation – Gift of God and Source of New Life. Documents from the Second European Ecumenical Assembly in Graz, Graz, Wien, Köln (Verlag Styria) 1998. A Third European Ecumenical Assembly is scheduled to take place in Sibiu (Romania) in September 2007.

It is in view of the need of the political institutions themselves and according to the self-understanding of churches that an organisation such as the Conference of European Churches, representing 125 churches from all over Europe, engages in dialogue with the European institutions. In bringing the voice of the voiceless to the institutions and serving the "common good", the churches' role might first and foremost be described as advocacy. In that, the churches defend their own interests as an institution in society and as a service provider in the public sphere, they might also be seen as lobbyists for their own (non-profit) interests.

Case Study 2: The Directive on Services in the Internal Market

In January 2004 the European Commission introduced a proposal for a Directive on Services in the Internal Market[126]. This Directive is a major element in the efforts of the EU Commission to make Europe "the most competitive and dynamic knowledge-based economy in the world"[127]. The Directive's intention is to eliminate obstacles to the freedom of establishment for service providers and the free movement of services between Member States of the European Union in order to accomplish the internal market of services. Thereby, the key element of the European Commission's original proposal was to introduce a "country of origin principle" i.e. that every service provider shall be allowed to offer its services in another country on the basis of the regulations in its homeland.

Churches and diaconal organisations are major providers of social services and healthcare services in many Member States of the European Union. The ways in which they provide such services depend upon the prevailing legal framework within the European Union and the Member States. With the Directive on Services in the Internal Market, they were facing the development of a new legal framework for the whole services sector. Regarding the first proposal of the Directive, the churches - together with many others - were very much concerned that this Directive would go much further than just eliminating the obstacles in the way of a genuine internal market for services. Privileging service providers from countries with lower salaries and lesser social standards would lead to a "race to the bottom" of social standards in the European Union. The churches were also concerned that social and healthcare services were only regarded under competition aspects, neglecting the specifics of person-related services in such sensitive sectors. Questions were raised about how quality elements of services like guarantee of provision of services, complete territorial coverage, effective accessibility, affordable prices, increase in choice, effective safety, security of supply and the protection of the environment could be integrated into the Directive.

[126] Proposal for a Directive of the European Parliament and of the Council on services in the internal market [SEC(2004) 21]. www.ec.europa.eu/internal_market/services/services-dir/
[127] Cf. Working together for growth and jobs. A new start for the Lisbon Strategy. Communication to the Spring European Council. Brussels, 02.02.2005. COM (2005) 24. P. 3. www.ec.europa.eu/growthandjobs/pdf/COM2005_024_en.pdf.

In a first step, the Church and Society Commission asked its member churches and member associations for a detailed description of services provided by churches and church related organisations in order to assess the possible impact of the Services Directive in the different European countries, focusing especially on the most vulnerable members in the societies. The results of this consultation process were handed over to the European Commission at a consultation on social services of general interest[128]. In a public reaction to the draft Services Directive in January 2005, the Church and Society Commission of the Conference of European Churches, together with Eurodiaconia[129], an Ecumenical federation of church-related non-statutory welfare organisations, explained its concerns on the proposed Directive, asking for an exemption of social and health services from the scope of the Directive. The statement also refers to the special role of churches as service providers: "The definition of services falling under the Directive should also consider the specific character of services provided by churches and diaconal organisations. The Community rules should respect their special characteristics as voluntary and non-profit enterprises, based on the commitment of church members."[130]

A permanent working group on social issues, consisting of specialists on social services from different member churches and supported by a working group of specialists on EU legislation, was coordinating the reaction of churches and diaconal organisations to the Services Directive. During the proceedings in the European Parliament, the Church & Society Commission was in a regular contact with the different rapporteurs of the political groups. In the days before the decisions in the Committee on Internal Market and Consumer affairs of the Parliament and the first reading in the Parliament, the Church and Society Commission, together with Eurodiaconia and the Roman Catholic partners from COMECE and Caritas Europa[131], addressed the members of the European Parliament with a "Common view", asking for an exclusion of social services and healthcare services from the scope of the Directive. A number of briefing papers and press releases published on the CEC website provided for public transparency of these activities.

Furthermore, the Church and Society Commission encouraged its member churches to contact their national governments about the concerns of the churches regarding the Services Directive[132]. On the occasion of the regular six monthly meetings with the Presidency of the European Union, the Church and Society Commission together with COMECE expressed its concern about the negative impact of the Services Directive on the quality of services and the preservation of social standards. Taking the many criticisms into account, the European Council specified in the

A joint answer from the Church and Society Commission of the Conference of European Churches and Eurodiaconia to the Questionnaire on Social Services of General Interest for the Social Protection Committee and the European Commission – 14 December 2004, http://www.ccc-kek.org/pdf/JointAnswer.pdf. ; Statement by Eurodiaconia and the Church & Society Commission of CEC regarding the Proposal for a directive on services in the internal market, 17 January 2005, www.cec-kek.org/content/economic.shtml. ; Caritas Europa is a confederation of 162 Roman-catholic relief, development and social service organisations, www.caritas-europa.org. ; www.cec-kek.org/pdf/CommonView.pdf.

conclusions of the Spring Summit in March 2005: "In order to promote growth and employment and to strengthen competitiveness, the internal market of services has to be fully operational while preserving the European social model. In the light of this ongoing debate which shows that the Directive as it is currently drafted does not fully meet these requirements, the European Council requests all efforts to be undertaken within the legislative process in order to secure a broad consensus that meets all these objectives."[133]

For the churches, it was important to make clear that the impact of the Services Directive would not be limited to the technical regulation of the internal market, but would have a major influence on the future shape of the European Social Model. To raise the awareness of this wider scope of the discussion, the Church and Society Commission together with Eurodiaconia in November 2005 organised an international consultation on "A Common vision for a social Europe: Towards quality of life for all." At that conference, Archbishop Karl Gustav Hammar from the Church of Sweden as well as Anna Diamantopoulou, former EU Commissioner for Employment and Social Affairs, expressed their concern about the reduction of the European Union to a common market model. Archbishop Hammar said: "As churches, we must move beyond comparison and competition, the win-lose race in the economic world, and emphasise what unites human beings, a basic value that is given and not won in competition, a common longing for peace and justice that is our only security and a willingness to share in order to grow together." Meetings with the Directors responsible for the European Commission on Social issues and Competition allowed discussion of the Services Directive in this broader perspective.

After more than two years of intense public debate, the second reading of the Services Directive in the European Parliament is still to come. At the moment, the Common Position of the European Commission and the Council of the European Union envisages an exclusion of most social services and healthcare services from the scope of the Directive. The highly controversial "country of origin principle" has been replaced by a "rule of the freedom to provide services".

During the whole period, the Church and Society Commission found itself in an internal discussion process on the objectives of its activities vis-à-vis the Services Directive: Is it the main task of the Church and Society Commission to defend the self-interests of churches and church-related service providers, taking into account the responsibility for more than half a million jobs of people employed by member churches and diaconal organisations in the field of social services and healthcare? Or are the churches and Diaconia wedded to a "privileged option for the

[133] Presidency conclusions, European Council Brussels 22 and 23 March 2005, Art. 22. http://ue.eu.int/ueDocs/cms_Data/docs/pressData/en/ec/84335.pdf.

poor", committed to advocate for the excluded, the marginalised people? So far, the different options have not turned out to be alternatives. We are convinced that churches and diaconal organisations may only have an interest to defend their structures as long as these structures serve the excluded and the marginalised.

7. Governments

Michael Aron, EU Director & Head of Scottish Executive EU Office, Brussels

The Scottish Executive EU Office (SEEUO) in Brussels was established in 1999 following the establishment of a Scottish Parliament and a new Scottish government (the Scottish Executive) with extensive devolved powers. We operate from premises on Rond Point Schuman known as 'Scotland House', which we share with Scotland Europa, a partnership of Scottish public, private and voluntary bodies.

The United Kingdom devolution settlement means that the UK government remains responsible for negotiating agreements in Brussels on all matters, including devolved matters. But EU law covers wide areas of devolved responsibility such as the environment, justice (Scotland has its own legal system), agriculture and fisheries and European legislation in these areas is implemented by the Scottish Parliament. Scotland also has significant interests in matters which are reserved, such as competition law and future financing, which have a major impact on devolved responsibilities.

We work very closely with the United Kingdom's Permanent Representation (UK-Rep). In fact, the EU offices for Scotland, Wales and Northern Ireland are formally part of UKRep and benefit from the same diplomatic status. This gives us excellent access to the Commission, the Council, European Parliament and all the other EU institutions.

Since 1999 we have developed a series of ways of making sure that Scottish interests are taken into account in EU negotiations:

First, there is the formal Memorandum of Understanding reached in 2001 between the UK government and the devolved administrations which includes a Concordat on Coordination of European Policy Issues. This is designed to ensure that Scottish (and Welsh and Northern Irish) interests are taken into account in the preparation of the United Kingdom's negotiating position in Brussels.

Second, there are informal arrangements between departments in Scotland and their London equivalents which ensure that Scottish officials and ministers can participate in detail in the preparation of United Kingdom positions.

Third, Scottish Ministers may attend Council meetings and Scottish officials may attend meetings of working groups. Our ministers will normally be present at key councils such as agriculture, fisheries, environment and justice and home affairs. They can and do speak – but their role, like that of officials at working groups, is to support and advance the single UK negotiating position, which they will have played a part in developing.

Fourth, using our contacts with the Commission, in the Council and with Members of the European Parliament to try to influence outcomes for Scotland in line with the UK position. We work particularly closely with the seven Scottish MEPs, who often pursue Scottish interests on a cross party basis.

Our key functions of the Scottish Executive EU Office can be described as:

- Gathering intelligence about forthcoming policy developments in the EU and the progress of existing policy proposals and helping Scottish Ministers and officials influence the development of proposals in line with UK negotiating objectives;
- Providing practical support to our Ministers and officials visiting Brussels;
- Working closely with the wide range of individuals and bodies representing Scottish interests (the Scottish MEPs, Scotland Europa, Scottish members of the Committee of the Regions and the Economic and Social Committee, representatives of Scottish local authorities and NGOs);
- Strengthening regional networks through involvement with the Committee of the Regions and through our relationships with many individual regions represented in Brussels particularly those with legislative competence;
- Promoting Scotland to the many EU communities represented in Brussels, through events, cultural activities, seminars, receptions. We aim to make a serious contribution to policy debate as well as to develop our contacts and promote a rounded view of Scotland.

Communication between Brussels and Scotland and involving stake-holders in the policy process is a vital aspect of our work. Taking account of our experience, Scottish First Minster, Jack McConnell and Commission Vice – President Margot Wallström in November 2005 agreed a "Building A Bridge" project which is looking at the Scottish Executive's experience of engaging with external stakehold-ers. The project was referred to in the Commission White Paper on Communication of February 2006. The conclusions of the project's various events and studies will be drawn together in a report which the Executive will submit to the European Commission in autumn 2006. It is hoped that the Scottish Executive's experience will help the Commission in developing upon and improving its own engage-ment with EU citizens.

Case Study: Bathing waters directive

The original Bathing Water Directive, agreed in 1976, was one of the first pieces of EU environmental legislation. In December 2000 the Commission adopted a communication to develop a new bathing water policy arguing that the Directive needed simplifying and updating, not least because of the improvements in science, information about bathing risks and imple-mentation of other directives protecting the water environment.

In October 2002 the Commission then adopted a proposal to revise the Directive. This original draft included an obligation to meet much tighter bathing water quality standards than the existing Bathing Water Direc-tive's very limited provisions for recreational waters (with no standards for these waters), some management measures for bathing waters and improved provision of information at bathing waters.

We had traditionally had a problem with the quality of bathing wa-ters in the south-west of Scotland, where the culmination of land type, agricultural land use and weather resulted in several bathing waters fail-ing after rain. We had already commissioned research to identify possible solutions to the problems we faced and we were moving forwards on several projects to address these, including co-sponsoring a project of-ficer for water resource management to help livestock farmers in Scotland minimise the threats from diffuse pollution.

One of the most important early steps for the Executive was to en-sure that Scotland's needs were fully incorporated in the UK line, because the UK Permanent Representation (UKRep) would be negotiating for the whole of the UK. Whilst the first reading was on-going, Executive policy colleagues discussed our needs with lobby groups, Scottish Water, the Scottish Environment Protection Agency (SEPA), local interest groups, local authorities, Scottish MEPs, Defra (the UK Department for Environment, Food and Rural Affairs), UKRep and members of the Commission about what we wished to include in the Directive in order to adequately protect the public, but also minimise the number of bathing waters failing in Scotland.

Our main issue focused on the need to be able to discount a sample after rain, particularly because the standards proposed were much more strict than those in the existing Directive (the minimum standard proposed in the revised Directive equated to the existing Directive's "excellent" status). Colleagues in SEPA devised a model that demonstrated a link between rainfall and the likelihood of a water sample failing to meet required standards over the next 24–48 hours, and we were able to use this to support our argument for samples being discounted.

This office played a key role in talking through the issues with our MEPs and in keeping them in the loop with what was going on in discussions between policy colleagues in Edinburgh and their Defra counterparts. As a result, during the first European Parliamentary reading, one of the Scottish MEPs tabled an amendment to meet Scottish concerns, most of which was adopted (and comes under Article 3(6)). Other important areas for Scotland were implementation of management measures, which we started trialing electronically during the 2003 bathing season.

Once the first reading had passed, although our key amendment had been included, it was important to keep all lines of communication open. Policy colleagues worked very closely with Defra. This office monitored discussions in working groups and in the Parliament, and provided advance information to colleagues in Edinburgh on what was going on (procedurally and as the policy was being developed).

This particular proposal went to conciliation, mainly because of differences between the Council and Parliament, one of which was the inclusion of a fourth category of water quality, "sufficient" (the original proposal had included "poor", "good" and "excellent"), which the Parliament felt went against the overall objective of the directive (to protect human health). This office kept policy colleagues in Scotland informed of these discussions as much as possible, and due to the network of contacts both within the Commission and Parliament, as well as external lobby groups it had developed, was in many cases able to provide officials with information more speedily than through the normal official channels.

The final Directive was formally adopted on 15 February 2006, was published in the Official Journal on 4 March 2006 and entered into force on 24 March 2006.

Another policy tool we have developed is a series of discussions called "Sub Rosa" from the practice in diplomacy during the Middle Ages of hanging a rose over a meeting as a sign of confidentiality and freedom to speak candidly. Our "Sub Rosa" is a high level, European policy discussion forum sponsored by an informal partnership between the Scottish Executive and the two government Development Agencies for Scotland - Scottish Enterprise and Highlands and Islands Enterprise.

The exercise is intended as a Scotland-led contribution to the EU policy formulation process. It is not directly part of any lobbying strategy. The aim is to provide a facility where senior officials have an opportunity - in an "off-the-record" setting - to ex-change views with colleagues from the EU institutions and from a wide range of Member States and regions.

Our most recent "Sub Rosa" took place on 1st December 2005 focusing on the clarity and transparency of EU legislation and its effects on businesses and in particular SMEs. The report and conclusions provided a contribution to the "Better Regulation" agenda. Previously we have discussed issues such as regional policy and state aids.

8. Law firms

Christian Duvernoy and Joerg Karenfort, Wilmer Hale, Brussels and Berlin

A Lawyer's Role in the EU Legislative Process – Lessons to Learn from a Transatlantic Perspective

Lawyers can play an important role in the legislative process. Sophisticated legal counsel can be critical in assessing risks in the legislative and policy arena in sufficient time so that a proper reaction can be designed. Lawyers familiar both with the industry sector and business strategy of their clients and the complex legislative process are in a unique position to provide strategic advice to identify risks for their clients and advise on the most effective strategies to pursue. This requires a thorough analysis of the legal aspects of what are often very technical issues as well as an in-depth understanding of applicable administrative and legislative procedures. Thus, lawyers can provide input on the legal implications of policy developments and analyse their background and context. Possible outputs for clients include legal and strategic studies of specific draft initiatives, plans for a coherent strategy that advances the client's interests in the specific legal and political context at issue, and drafts of specific legislative language that can be put forward in the legislative process. Lawyers also assist in coordinating teams to deal with legislative or policy issues that may include public relations or communications professionals, in addition to the spokespersons for or high-ranking executive of their client.

8.1. The US perspective

Legal and strategic advice in the public policy arena has a long tradition in the United States. Major Washington law firms are often engaged by clients to assist on legislative initiatives in reaction to key policy developments. This tradition is based in part on the propensity of the US political and governmental system to address policy issues through legal and regulatory solutions, rather than an informally agreed approach among the major stakeholders. This results from (i) the more arm's length and at times adversarial relationship between the government and industry; (ii) the complex structure of a federal governmental system that limits Presidential authority through checks and balances both at federal and local (state) levels, and in which independent administrative agencies have powerful roles to play; and (iii) the constitutionalisation of many policy issues in the US. As a result, lawyers are in demand both in government and in the private sector, with prominent attorneys often moving back and forth between positions in government and the private sector. Strict codes apply to safe-guard against conflicts of interest and there is a high degree of transparency about the roles in which lawyers are acting. The "revolving door" between the public and private sectors enhances the ability of those involved to understand the political, institutional and business concerns of the other side. It also leads naturally to close contacts between lawyers in the private sector and their former colleagues in government and administrative agencies. These contacts are helpful both in obtaining access to decision makers and in overcoming initial suspicion on the part of public officials of the motives of their private sector interlocutors.

8.2 The EU perspective

Law firms with major practices in legislative and policy work have long been present in Brussels. According to official estimates, there are about 15,000 "lobbyists" in Brussels, comprised mainly of public affairs and public relations consultants, representatives of trade associations, NGOs, or members of the government relations offices of major corporations that maintain a presence in Brussels. Only a small fraction of this number is composed of lawyers. This is not surprising, since law firms involved in legislative and policy work typically play a more technical role that is distinct from that of political lobbyists or campaigners/communications specialists. In Brussels, a lawyer's experience in analysing and resolving complex legal and administrative issues, combined with an understanding of the policy questions at issue in what is typically a regulated sector, as well as a sense of the politics at play can provide clients with added value.

The institutional climate in Brussels means that lawyers can play a particularly effective role on legislative and policy issues. The EU institutions are lightly staffed compared to national administrations. Access to decision makers, including Members of the European Parliament, is relatively open and straightforward. European officials and Parliamentarians generally welcome expert external advice on the issues they are dealing with. Lawyers can provide this by translating the business concerns of their clients into the appropriate European legislative and administrative framework for the officials and Parliamentarians involved in the legislative process, while remaining sensitive to the overall political climate in regard to the relevant issue. Experienced Brussels-based advocates can also assist in reducing any "institutional distrust" of the private sector that there may be on the part of European officials. They often have established reputations in a given subject matter area in their own right and, if they have been practicing for some time in Brussels, their integrity will be a known quality for their institutional contacts.

In addition, a revolving door has been evolving in Brussels since the 1990s. It is usually one-way from the institutions into the private sector, however, since it is still much more rare than in the US for prominent lawyers to be recruited into the senior European civil service from private practice. Nevertheless, skilled lawyers with significant experience in the European institutions can be found more frequently among Brussels law firms. In this context, it is important for clients to choose with care the right legal advisor for a particular issue.

8.3 The EU Member States' perspective

In the domestic (Member State) legislative context it has been less frequent than at EU level to find practicing lawyers that specialise in legislative and public policy work. Law firms in most Member States have confined their activities to those of a traditional legal counsel.

It has not least been the arrival of US-based law firms in a number of Member State markets that has helped to begin to change mindsets. These firms have brought their legislative and public policy experience and approach with them and are increasingly convincing clients of the added value their lawyers can bring to bear on an issue. Each national legislative system has its own specific features that make it difficult to make general statements about the role lawyers play in national legislative and policy arenas. The general principles outlined above in regard to EU legislative work also apply at national level. Clients in direct contact with national authorities have a specific need for precise legal drafting to deal with technical issues in the legislative process. Lawyers at national level can assist here in translating the strategic goals of their clients into operational legal language.

8.4 Transatlantic Interdependencies

In our increasingly globalised world, transatlantic coordination between regulators and agencies is growing. European regulators will look across the ocean for approaches to an issue that have been taken in the US and vice versa. Comparing different approaches to the same problem on both sides of the Atlantic can also inspire new solutions. This creates significant opportunities for coordinated legislative and policy action by industry. Law firms that are at home in both the US and European legislative and administrative systems can capitalise on their experience to provide coordinated support to clients that nevertheless takes account of the institutional and political specificities of each side of the Atlantic.

Concrete examples of close cooperation between European and American regulatory authorities already exist. Competition authorities as well as financial market regulators are in close touch with one another on specific proceedings. More generally, regulators in sensitive policy areas such as trade, the environment or the communications sector at times may draw inspiration or at least obtain education in regard to a specific approach to an issue from each other. Transatlantic regulatory cooperation can be not only a risk but also a major opportunity for industry. Again, lawyers with experience in the regulatory and policy environments in both the US and Europe can help their clients make a difference on transatlantic issues.

8.5 A Case Study

The following case study provides an example of the role lawyers can play to assist their clients in the EU legislative process. Large parts of this process involved highly technical legal issues on which the traditional analytical and drafting skills of lawyers were able to be put to good use. While the legal input involved was part of a larger political and policy strategy, it played a key role in the legislative initiative and contributed to a successful outcome for the client.

In April 2005, three months before the European Parliament's vote at second reading on the Council's Common Position on the Computer Im-plemented Inventions ("CII") Directive, we were asked by a leading open source software developer to assist in lobbying Parliament. Our client was seeking amendments to the Common Position that would make it more difficult to obtain patents on computer programmes as such and ensure that all software developers would be required to share interoperability infor-mation to allow software from different vendors to work together, even if their software was patented. The Council's Common Position had rejected practically all of Parliament's amendments at first reading. The Common Position presented a real threat that software patents would become easier to obtain and much more wide-spread.

We worked at three levels: Through an industry coalition of software and hardware companies; in alliance with another major software de-veloper that shared our client's positions; and directly on behalf of our client. Although it was late in the legislative process, the particular cir-cumstances of how the Member States had agreed their Common Position as well as the Parliament's composition having changed due to the 2004 elections meant that Parliament was keen to re-examine most of the key provisions in the second reading.

The legal background was crucial in this context. Our client argued that software, which is already protected by copyright, should not be pat-entable unless it makes a technical contribution to a field of technology/ applied natural science. At the same time, we had to take into account that, over the past decade, software, and even business methods, have become more easily patentable, especially in the United States.

This was not necessarily an issue on which positions were based on political ideology. The free software movement, with which open source software development is associated, did find more support among left-oriented and green MEPs. But our client was a for-profit corporation that developed open source software and sold software services to large cor-porations, public administrations and universities worldwide. Our mission was also therefore to explain to center-right and liberal MEPs why in-creased patent protection for software would be bad for the industry and ultimately bad for the economy.

While we also met with the legal advisors to the main political groups, our discussions with key MEPs and their cabinets primarily focused on these technical and economic implications. Some of these meetings took place within the framework of the industry trade association.

By contrast, other steps in our action plan were purely legal. In advance of a key vote of the Legal Affairs Committee on the amendments it would propose to the entire Parliament, we worked together with our allies and "friendly MEPs" or their cabinets to draft compromise texts that could be adopted as amendments. Since various circles of allies had differing degrees of support for our client's position, we developed different versions of amendments, ranging from the "pure" positions of our client to a "lowest common denominator" version that could be accepted by all in the trade association.

Getting through amendments to a Common Position is difficult as at second reading the Parliament must act by an absolute majority of its 732 members – on the first reading, it acts by majority of votes cast. After the Legal Affairs' vote, in the weeks leading up to the plenary Parliament vote, we therefore prepared a number of submission papers for prominent MEPs and analysed all of the 178 amendments that had been tabled.

The full European Parliament debated the draft directive in early July 2005 in Strasbourg.

The night before the debate, we drafted a final position paper for a sympathetic MEP who was scheduled to speak on the Parliament floor the next day. In the chaotic environment of a Parliament plenary, our response reached the MEP at the last minute and was picked up only in part. At the same time, we prepared detailed tables for all the MEPs indicating which of the 178 amendments we supported and indicating our preferred versions of different amendments.

In an ironic twist before the vote each side in the debate found common agreement in a negative option. Since, each amendment to the Common Position required an absolute majority of MEPs and because MEPs and their groups were divided on the issues, neither side was confident of a majority on all of the key elements of the legislation. The compromise was therefore to unite in rejecting, by an absolute majority, the text of the Common Position. This killed the legislative proposal, but was the second-best outcome for our client – better no directive at all than a harmful directive.

This was the first time that the Parliament had ever voted to reject a Council Common Position in its entirety at second reading. Normally the Parliament would be expected to put forward its own amendments and differences between the two institutions would be ironed out in the "conciliation" procedure. The Parliament's website proclaimed its vote as a "historic victory".

At the same time as we tried to put forward our arguments in Parliament, we also contacted the more influential Commission DGs and what we thought might be key Member States. If the Directive had gone back to the Council and into the conciliation procedure, we needed every ally that we could muster. We also believed that Member State Governments would be able to influence key MEPs. While the issues did not divide them along national lines, industry groups from particular countries were heavily lobbying their own MEPs.

In comparison to some companies on the other side, our client had invested in a highly focused but shoestring-budgeted legislative effort at the very last minute. We fielded a small team in which, we believe, our presence as lawyers was significant. Other companies were able to employ more lobbyists but our client's recognition of the legal difficulties inherent in this debate greatly contributed to a successful outcome.

9. PR firms

Caroline Wunnerlich and Bernd Buschhausen,
Fleishman-Hillard, Brussels and Berlin

Aluminium for future generations –
An initiative of the European aluminium industry

9.1 Introduction
Lobbying, public affairs, government relations, corporate communications and many other definitions all belong to the catalogue of services that most consultancies provide in Brussels. Many lobbying case studies therefore choose to focus on a particular piece of legislation that can be neatly mapped from start to finish with arrows showing points of influence. The reality is, however, that lobbying and its related definitions cover a broad range of activity that is often not limited to specific legislative influence. Over the years, the fundamental challenges of defining who you are within an EU context, how you are perceived, what you contribute, and how to get your voice heard all form the basis of much consultancy work. Maastricht, Nice, Enlargement - the EU arena has become so increasingly complex over the last decade, the agenda increasingly wide-ranging, the countries and players so numerous, that establishing voice and credibility above the crowd is an imperative prerequisite to any successful lobbying activity.

9.2 Starting Point

Such was the experience of the aluminium industry in the late 1990s. With sustainability and climate change debates raging, the industry had begun to notice that there was a wide degree of ignorance or misperception about its activity and contribution to the environment. A perception audit undertaken with policy-makers and influencers in 1997 had confirmed the ambivalence that dominated impressions:

• Aluminium was considered a modern and innovative material, but was viewed as being harmful to the environment in both its production and waste management.
• Aluminium's potential contribution to sustainable development was not known or appreciated by important decision makers in the EU's political and social arena.

Moreover, the negative image of the material in the stakeholder arena had limited the industry's influence and ability to participate in the ongoing context of the new focus on sustainable development policies across Europe. The major wake-up calls came when the City of Berlin public procurement authorities decided to ban aluminium from its catalogue of specified construction materials, and when the Danish government 'can ban' was introduced and threatened to spread to other EU markets. Competitive materials were also becoming more aggressive: important market share in the beverage packaging domain had begun to be threatened by innovative PET bottles, and the steel industry had mounted an impressive promotion campaign in key automotive and constructive sectors on the theme of 'Made of Steel.' It was at this point that the seven major aluminium producers in Europe agreed on the need for concerted action with external help. A consultancy brief was issued and Fleishman-Hillard in Brussels won a competitive pitch to provide a programme to address the aluminium industry's image with opinion formers and decision makers in Brussels and in six key markets (UK, France, Germany, Belgium, Italy and the Netherlands).

9.3 Objectives

The objective of this Europe-wide initiative was to enhance the image of the industry and give it a credible voice with environmental policy-makers at European and national level. The theme of communications activities was centered around Sustainable Development and aluminium's positioning within this debate. Given the aluminium industry's many ecological advantages over other materials, it was critical to get the industry engaged with policy-makers and to have its views acknowledged in the decision making process. In order to emphasise its environmental responsibility, the industry focused on the conclusions of the Rio conference in 1992 and the Agenda 21 which became the basis for dialogue between industry, politicians, functionaries and NGOs on the subject of sustainability. Aluminium's contribution to this debate was not obvious. Considered energy-guzzling to produce and problematic to dispose of, the industry had to focus on communicating its environmental benefits while addressing their stakeholders' concerns head-on.

9.4 Strategic Approach

Communicating benefits while still addressing concerns is a challenging objective. The approach was therefore not one of just 'telling', but most importantly one of being seen to be 'listening'. In order to build dialogue systematically with various stakeholders, the programme was structured in three phases over three years:

In order to make absolutely clear the industry's commitment to focusing on the issues under the broad umbrella of sustainable development, the programme was also given a distinctive title and logo which still hold today: Aluminium for Future Generations.

9.5 The Process: From Consultation to Real Results

The goal of the communication activity was to position the industry as a credible partner by participating in a constructive, candid and results-oriented debate. A specific approach was developed to structure this debate in a pan-European context which mirrored EU policy-making. First, a European industry Consultation Paper was developed along the lines of a Commission 'Green Paper' that invited interested parties to give views on the issues at stake around aluminium and sustainable development. This initiative in itself was a first for the industry and sent a strong signal of openness and partnership to external audiences. Secondly, consultation meetings were organised between industry and the interested parties to share and discuss these views in a Roundtable forum. Representatives from ministries, political parties and NGOs were invited to participate at both Brussels and national level in all six countries. Thirdly, the industry took the strategic priorities for sustainable development that emerged from the consultations and developed a series of industry commitments for the future. These commitments were to address in concrete terms issues such as recycling quotas and production methods and to report back in an ongoing dialogue with the stakeholders.

9.6 Results

After four years of internal and external consultancy advice from Fleishman-Hillard, the Aluminium for Future Generations campaign had established itself as the central communications platform for the European aluminium industry in Europe. Rather than being perceived as yet another 'PR slogan', the campaign was seen as credible and substantive with a commitment to addressing issues and making improvements. Another key success was the fact that, for the first time, the highly competitive players of the aluminium industry were engaging in a one-voice-strategy across Europe. The programme helped to raise the efficiency of industry communications both as a corporate component as well as at association levels. As a result, the industry was regularly invited by government and other opinion formers to give views on issues and became seen as a partner for political dialogue. Today, aluminium industry representatives are regularly featured as high level contributors to major policy conferences and debates across Europe.

Furthermore, the discussions also triggered a number of scientific studies and co-operation projects between industry, NGOs and academia. Given the increasing influence of both the latter interest groups on policy-making, this co-operation became a real pillar for collaboration and building relationships. Instead of being attacked as the 'enemy', the industry became part of the solution.

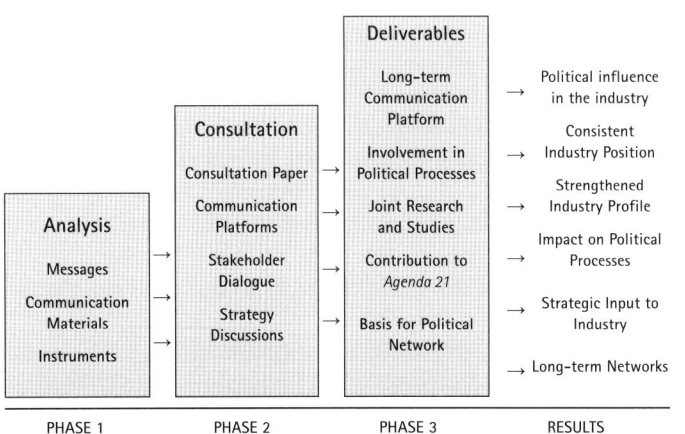

Finally, the Aluminium for Future Generations initiative launched a new dynamic and set benchmarks internally with its members that changed old mindsets and set them on a path of long-term proactive public affairs and issue management for the future. A whole section on the European Aluminium Association website is dedicated to the campaign, outlining its goals, ongoing work and relevant events.

9.7 Conclusion

The Aluminium for Future Generations initiative was started before the new millennium, but it remains a highly relevant case study of best practice in effective long-term public affairs. It takes all the ingredients of an old-fashioned industrial sector, relying on well-trodden paths with customers and practices, and not heeding warning signals from its regulatory and commercial environment. Along comes a major policy focus such as sustainable development, and the industry finds itself on the defensive, without allies, and without a voice. Only by embarking on a process of real change and commitment, with CEO endorsement and investment of time and money, could it chart a path out of its corner. The Aluminium for Future Generations programme demonstrates the importance of a strong consistent communication approach towards political audiences in Europe:

- Only when you reach out to players both at European and national levels, with the same set of messages and positions, will you be able to generate the necessary impact on the policy-making process.
- Industry communications must be based on concrete actions in order to fulfil expectations and claims made in stated positions. Demands made during the policy dialogue have to be backed up by deliverables that underline commitment to the process.
- Communications with policy makers have to take into account that what you say in one Member State may impact your ability to act in another. Business needs to consolidate its messaging across Europe in order to protect its credibility with all EU stakeholders.

In conclusion, Aluminium for Future Generations shows that good public affairs management can work, but that it is a long-term approach – and not a short-term 'image' fix – that effects real change.

$\rightarrow$

Country	Timing of events	Event
	20 January 1999	European Commission DG XI–Environment Roundtable.
	10 January 1999	European Commission DG III–Industry Roundtable.
	3 February 1999	Greenmelt in Duffel: site visit and roundtable with Flemish governmental and academic audiences.
	5 February 1999	Clervaugh in Luxembourg: site visit and round-table with Walloon governmental, political and academic audiences.
	11 March 1999	Site visits and roundtable about recycling with political and governmental audiences (Compiègne/Isle les Meldeuse).
	1 April 1999	Site visits and roundtable about aluminium in automobile with political and governmental audiences (Compiègne/Le Havre).
	9–10 December 1998	Seminar with NGOs (political foundations, environmental NGOs, Church).
	8 February 1999	Political dinner: representatives from the Bundesrat (Environmental Committee, Federal and State Ministries of Environment and Economy).
	3 March 1999	Political dinner: CDU/CSU. FDP parliamentary groups.
	28 April 1999	NGO seminar (environmental NGOs and think tanks).
	F16 June 1999	Political dinner: SPD, Greens parliamentary groups.
	28 November 1998	Informal one-to-one testing of targets and hand out of Consultation Document.
	28 January 1999	Informal one-to-one testing of targets and hand out of Consultation Document.
	18 February 1999	Recycling Roundtable.
	19 February 1999	Energy Roundtable.
	13 April 1999	Recycling Event – Visit to Vedani's Factory.
	3 May 1999	Energy saving Event – Visit to Alcoa's smelter.
	25 January 1999	Roundtable.
	29 January 1999	Roundtable (both with Dutch Governmental, NGO, Political & Academic audiences).
	21 October 1998	House of Commons. Parliamentary seminar.
	3 March 1999	Roundtable with Parliamentarians chaired by Trade and Industry Minister John Battle.
	10 March 1999	Seminar with DETR/DTI Government officials.
	22/23 March 1999	Visit to Aluminium smelter with all-party group of Parliamentarians.
	30 March 1999	NGO Consultation Roundtable.
	30 March 1999	2nd Roundtable with Parliamentarians chaired by Environment Minister Michael Meacher.
	15 March 1999	Meeting with Swiss Federation, members of Parliament and NGOs.

Source: EAA, Response of the Aluminium Industry to the Consultation
(http://www.eaa.net/future/response.asp)

VI. Outlook

Outlooks into the future are always difficult and in some cases are nothing more than a look into the crystal ball. But EU lobbying in general is not so much different from lobbying in other world capitals, like Washington[134] (even though some EU lobbyists will tell you so for obvious reasons). Therefore, we assume that:

- Lobbying will continue to expand and to fragment as more and more stakeholders – including governments on all levels – see the need to have a presence in the political capital.
- This expansion will not be due only to new interests entering the political fray. If past trends continue, much will be a result of stakeholders beginning to lobby on their own as well as continuing to belong to a trade association or other umbrella lobbying group. This will primarily be because the specific needs of many groups and organisations cannot be entirely met by an umbrella lobbying organisation.
- It will become more and more important – especially for those new to the lobbying scene – to use a lobbying firm or some other entity that can help the stakeholder plan and work his way through the increasingly complex and complicated processes and interconnections that characterise lobbying.
- The localities (cities, towns, regions) will become increasingly important in their lobbying since issues shift to the regional level in many cases.
- Policy issues are likely to become less and less compartmentalised, i.e. issues like health care will continue to affect more and more stakeholders and not just health care groups such as pharmaceutical companies, doctors and hospitals. In short, many issues will spread out to other areas where you do not expect them at first glance.
- The growth of coalition building is likely to continue and reach new levels. A coalition is fast becoming the only way to mount a lobbying effort that stands a chance of success, given the increased competition among stakeholders for the ear of the policy makers. Most of these coalitions will be ad hoc, on one issue only, and will disband after the issue is won or lost. Increasingly, also, these coalitions include strange bedfellows such as trade unions together

[134] Harris/Fleisher, The Handbook of Public Affairs, p. 316

with business groups, animal rights groups together with pharmaceutical companies, among many others, because these coalitions suit a certain need at a certain time.

- Entrepreneurial spirit will rise to meet the challenge of these developments by stakeholders and lobbyists refining old lobbying techniques and developing new ones based on new technologies – like the Internet has given rise to weblogs - to be competitive in the lobbying game.

EU lobbying will further have to be seen in its context of global lobbying strategies[135]:

- In the US, as well as being a multibillion dollar based business around Washington, lobbying has also its equivalent epicenters around each state government and international operations focused on the World Trade Organization (WTO) and World Bank.
- In the EU, as discussed, the bulk of the coordination of EU activity is centered on Brussels, with major activities also being focused on the prime EU capitals, London, Paris and Berlin being particularly significant. Other lobbying centres are growing, as with Geneva because of the WTO.
- In Australia there is a well developed lobbying industry around Melbourne and Canberra.
- After the fall of the iron curtain, new lobbying centres have been developing only recently, including Moscow, Prague and Warsaw.
- The development of China's naturally nascent lobbying industry is focused on key entry points such as Singapore, Shanghai, Beijing and Hong Kong, being a major focus for the next lobbying decade.
- Similar explorations of major lobbying markets such as Delhi, Mumbai and Bangalore in India and Tokyo in Japan are on their way.
- EU-Africa relations will become a major issue. The EU lobbying by African governments both for development aid and for opening the EU market with regard to their natural resources will gain in importance as it has in the US.

EU lobbyists will have to take into account much more in the future one fact, whether as a company representative, as a consultant or in another of the described lobbyist functions: they cannot act isolated

[135] Harris/Fleisher, The Handbook of Public Affairs, p. 561

but they are part of a global lobbying agenda. Consequently, EU lobbying will be a strategic core business function for companies and all other stakeholders that wish to compete successfully and operate internationally in the future, since EU lobbying will be at the leading edge of complex governmental EU policies and respective stakeholder demands.

As a result, EU lobbying will develop to become a job category of its own, as its counterpart in the US has been for a long time already. While in today's EU, people from different educational backgrounds - like law, political science, public relations, engineering, economy etc. - move into lobbying more or less accidentally, tomorrow's EU will see a professional species of its own. There will be specific university studies and diplomas for lobbying in Brussels as there are university courses and postgraduate master degrees for lobbying in Washington. Already today, some public and private universities in Brussels and the Member State capitals offer such postgraduate courses to a small extent. Since lobbying is a high-end management task, it demands certain qualifications that are rather rare. You need to have a combination of factual knowledge and analytical skills on the one hand, while on the other hand, you need to have an outgoing personality. Lobbying is not about being a gourmet. Nor is it helpful to be a bookworm.

It is for the rare combination of these facts that stakeholders will pay you extraordinary salaries or fees when you lobby their interests. In the US, being a lobbyist is one of the most lucrative jobs. External lobbyists there either charge an hourly rate of up to $ 800.-, which is comparable to the top law firms, or an annual retainer of between $ 200.000.- and $ 1.000.000.-. Internal lobbyists' salaries – like the ones of the company General Counsels – are company management level and often reach an amount of over $ 500.000.- before bonus. To be able to compete with the lobbying of third countries, e.g. the US, the benchmarks for EU lobbyists will soon develop accordingly. The combination of the interesting, demanding and speedy environment of the job and the very competitive remuneration will also attract top personnel for those jobs in the EU. So becoming a lobbyist in the EU will probably be one of the most exciting job opportunities in the future.

Tip

As a future EU lobbyist, you need the following qualifications:

- Analytical skills
- Expert knowledge
- Multilingualism
- Multiculturalism
- Credibility
- Empathy
- Discretion
- Self-assurance

VII. Lobbying lexicon

Accreditation: the process of formally registering as a lobbyist with the EU institutions

Badge: access pass to the EU institutions

Code of conduct: a set of rules to guide behaviour with regard to the EU institutions.

Comitology: it refers to the committee system, which oversees the acts implemented by the Commission. The committees, which are forums for discussion, are made up of representatives from Member States and are chaired by the Commission. They ensure that the Commission is able to establish a dialogue with national administrations before implementing measures. The Commission ensures that they reflect, as far as possible, the situation in each country in question.

Coreper: the Member States' permanent representatives meet weekly within the Permanent Representatives Committee (Coreper). The role of this committee is to prepare the work of the Council, with the exception of most agricultural issues, which are handled by the Special Committee on Agriculture. A number of working groups, made up of officials from the national administrations, assists Coreper.

Decision: an instrument by which the EU institutions give a ruling on a particular matter. By means of a decision, the institutions can require a Member State or a citizen of the EU to take or refrain from taking a particular action, or confer rights or impose obligations on a Member State or a citizen. A decision is an individual measure, and the persons to whom it is addressed must be specified individually, which distinguishes a decision from a regulation.

Directive: an EU directive is a frame law, addressed to the Member States. Its main purpose is to align national legislation. A directive is binding on the Member States as to the result to be achieved but leaves them the choice of the form and method they adopt to realise the objectives within the framework of their internal legal order. If a directive has not been transposed into national legislation in a

Member State, if it has been transposed incompletely or if there is a delay in transposing it, citizens can directly invoke the directive in question before the national courts.

EU: the European Union is a supranational union of currently 25 democratic member states from the European continent. The European Union was established under that name in 1992 by the Treaty on European Union (the Maastricht Treaty). However, many aspects of the Union existed before that date through a series of predecessor relationships, dating back to 1951. The Union nowadays has a common single market consisting of a customs union, a single currency managed by the European Central Bank (so far adopted by 12 of the 25 member states), a Common Agricultural Policy, a common trade policy, and a Common Fisheries Policy. A Common Foreign and Security Policy was also established as the second of the three pillars of the European Union. The Schengen Agreement abolished passport control, and customs checks were also abolished at many of the EU's internal borders, creating a single space of mobility for EU citizens to live, travel, work and invest.

Gatekeeper: a person who guards or monitors passage to the relevant EU decision maker.

Government Relations: other word for lobbying describing a management discipline at the interface of politics, economy and society. It has both elements of legal counsel and PR, though being a discipline of its own. It is about relationships with governments and parliaments, therefore the name "government relations".

Grassroots: a political movement for individual constituents of a community to voice their ideas and opinions. The movement allows citizens to organise through a bottom-up approach with voters demanding change, rather than existing political leaders directing the process in a top-down fashion.

Lobbying: the professional practice of public affairs or government relations advocacy, with the goal of influencing a governing body by promoting a point of view.

Lobbyist: a person who professionally influences legislation as well as public opinion. Many major corporations, associations, NGOs and other political interest groups hire professional lobbyists to promote their interests as intermediaries. Others maintain in-house government relations or public affairs departments. Think tanks aim to lobby through regular releases of detailed reports and supporting research to the media for dissemination.

Monitoring: method for obtaining political intelligence with regard to EU legislation by going through agendas, press, communications etc. to find what is relevant for your purposes.

NGO: a non-governmental organisation is a non-profit group or association that acts outside of institutionalised political structures and pursues matters of interest to its members by lobbying, persuasion, or direct action. The term is generally restricted to social, cultural, legal, and environmental advocacy groups having goals that are primarily non-commercial. NGOs usually gain at least a portion of their funding from private sources.

Permanent Representation: each Member State has a Permanent Representation in Brussels that represents it and defends its national interest at EU level. The head of each representation is the country's ambassador to the EU. These ambassadors ("permanent representatives") meet weekly within the Permanent Representatives Committee (Coreper).

Public affairs: a catch-all term that includes public policy as well as public administration, both of which are closely related to and draw upon the fields of political science as well as economics. Usually used as a synonym for lobbying.

Public policy: a course of action or inaction chosen by public authorities to address a problem. Public policy is expressed in the body of laws, regulations, decisions and actions of government.

Regulation: an EU regulation is in fact a law, i.e. a general measure that is binding in all its parts. Unlike directives, which are addressed to the Member States, and decisions, which are for specified recipients, regulations are addressed to everyone. A regulation is directly applicable, which means that it creates law which takes immediate effect in all the Member States in the same way as a national law, without any further action on the part of the national authorities.

Stakeholder: person or organisation that has a legitimate interest in a project or entity. In discussing the decision making process for institutions - including large business corporations, government agencies and non-profit organisations - the concept has been broadened to include everyone with an interest (or "stake") in what the entity does.

Think tank: a research institute, other organisation or informal group providing advice and ideas on any aspect of future planning and strategy - for example issues of policy, commerce, and military interest, often associated with military laboratories, corporations, academia, or other institutions. Usually this term refers specifically to organisations, which support multidisciplinary theorists, and intellectuals who endeavor to produce analysis or policy recommendations.

Trialogue: an informal, tripartite meeting between the Parliament, the Council and the Commission after the Second Reading in the co-decision legislative procedure.

Workshop: a gathering or training session, which may be several days in length. It emphasises problem-solving, hands-on training, and requires the involvement of the participants.

VIII. Subject index

IX. Index of people

X. References

R. Scott Appleby, The Ambivalence of the Sacred - Religion, Violence, and Reconciliation, Rowman and Littlefield, Lanham, Boulder, New York, Oxford, 2000

Gunnar Bender and Lutz Reulecke: Handbuch des deutschen Lobbyisten. Wie ein modernes und transparentes Politikmanagement funktioniert, F.A.Z Institut, Frankfurt, 2003, p. 117

Pieter Bouwen, A comparative study of business lobbying in the European Parliament, the European Commission and the Council of Ministers, MPIfG Discussion Paper 02/7, Max-Planck-Institut für Gesellschaftsforschung, Cologne, November 2002

Pieter Bouwen, Corporate Lobbying in the European Union: Towards a Theory of Access, European University Institute, Firenze, 2001.

Burson-Marsteller, The Definitive Guide to Lobbying the European Institutions, Brussels, 2005

The Church and Society Commission of the Conference of European Churches, the Evangelical Church in Germany and the Commission of the Bishops' Conferences of the European Community: The European Convention: The Evolution of a Constitution for Europe, Joint documentation, Brussels 2003

Grace Davie, Religion in Modern Europe. A Memory Mutates, Oxford, Oxford University Press, 2000

Hermann Denz (ed.), Die europäische Seele -Leben und Glauben in Europa, Czernin, Vienna, 2002

Documents from the Second European Ecumenical Assembly in Graz Reconciliation – Gift of God and Source of New Life, Styria, Graz, Vienna, Cologne, 1998

Justin Greenwood, Interest representation in the European Union, Palgrave Macmillan, Basingstoke, 2003

Phil Harris and Craig S. Fleisher, The Handbook of Public Affairs, Sage Publications Ltd., London, 2005

David Herbert, Religion and Civil Society – Rethinking Public Religion in the Contemporary World, Ashgate, Burlington, 2004

Andreas Jobst: Foreign Lobbying in the U.S. – A Latin American Perspective, London School of Economics and Political Science, London, 2002

Ulrich H.J. Körtner, Wiederkehr der Religion? Das Christentum zwischen neuer Spiritualität und Gottvergessenheit, Gütersloher Verlagshaus, Gütersloh, 2006

Christian Lahusen and Claudia Jauß: Lobbying als Beruf - Interessengruppen in der Europäischen Union, Nomos Verlag, Baden-Baden, 2001

Otto Lerbinger, Corporate Public Affairs: interacting with interest groups, media and government, Lawrence Erlbaum Associates, New Jersey, 2006

Local Governments Network of Central and Eastern European Countries, CEEC Logon, Report 2002: Lobbying in Europe, A Challenge for Local and Regional Governments, Association of Austrian Cities and Towns, Vienna, 2002

Theodore Lowi: The End of Liberalism: The Second Republic of the United States, W. W. Norton, 2nd edition, New York, 1979

Valeria Marziali, Lobbying in Brussels, Discussion Paper C 155, Center for European Integration Studies, Bonn, 2006

Irina Michalowitz: Service bureaux of decision-makers or successful spin-doctors: Assessing interest group influence in the EU and the US, in: European Union Studies Association (EUSA), Biennial Conference, March - April 2005, p.2

Lester W. Milbrath: The Washington Lobbyists, Rand McNally, Chicago, 1963

Office for Official Publications of the European Communities, How the European Union works: your guide to the EU institutions, Luxembourg, 2005

Official documentation of the European Ecumenical Assembly Basel, Switzerland, 15-21 May, 1989: Peace with Justice, Geneva 1989

Rinus van Schendelen, Machiavelli in Brussels, The Art of Lobbying the EU, 4th printing, Amsterdam University Press, Amsterdam, 2004

Kay Lehman Schlozman and John T.Tierney: Organised Interests and American Democracy, Harper and Row, New York, 1986

Jeffrey A. Segal, Charles M. Cameron, and Albert D. Cover: A Special Model of Roll Call Voting: Senators, Constituents, Presidents and Interest Groups in Supreme Court Confirmations, American Journal of Political Science 36, 1992, p.96-121

Mark A. Smith: American Business and Political Power: Public Opinion, Elections and Democracy, University of Chicago Press, Chicago, 2000

Richard A. Smith: Interest Group Influence in the US Congress", Legislative Studies Quarterly 20, 1995, p.89-139

Lee Staples, Roots to power: a manual for grassroots organizing, Praeger publishers, Westport, Connecticut, 2004

Alex Warleigh and Jenny Fairbrass: Influence and Interests in the European Union: The New Politics of Persuasion and Advocacy, Europa Publications, London, 2002

John R. Wright: Interest Groups & Congress: Lobbying Contributions and Influence, Allyn and Bacon, Boston 1996

XI. About the Author

Dr. Andreas Geiger has been an attorney and legal lobbyist for his entire professional career. He has been consulting and representing major clients in almost all EU policy areas with the European Commission and the European Parliament, as well as in the national governments and parliaments of the EU Member States. He further is a visiting professor for EU law at the University of Düsseldorf.

Starting in the cabinet of the Advocate General at the European Court of Justice, he became an attorney at the law firm Wessing, Head of the EU Law Center of Ernst & Young, President & CEO of the lobbying firm Cassidy & Associates Europe, and is a founding partner of the lobbying focused law firm Alber & Geiger.

He holds a law degree and an EU law doctorate from the University of Tübingen, along with a European Masters degree from the University of Bonn.